Taxcafe.co.uk Tax Guides

How to Avoid
Inheritance Tax

By Carl Bayley BSc ACA

Important Legal Notices:

TAXCafe™
TAX GUIDE – "How to Avoid Inheritance Tax"

Published by:
Taxcafe UK Limited
4 Polwarth Gardens
Edinburgh EH11 1LW
Tel: (01592) 560081

Email address: team@taxcafe.co.uk

First Edition   May 2003
Second Edition April 2004

ISBN 1 904608 12 4

Copyright

Trademarks

Disclaimer

About the Author

Carl Bayley is the author of a number of tax guides designed specifically for the layman. Carl's particular speciality is his ability to take the weird, complex and inexplicable world of taxation and set it out in the kind of clear, straightforward language that taxpayers themselves can understand. As he often says, 'my job is to translate tax into English'.

Carl takes the same approach when speaking on taxation, a role he has undertaken with some relish on a number of occasions, including his highly acclaimed series of seminars at the Evening Standard Homebuyer Show.

In addition to being a recognised author and speaker on the subject, he has also spoken on property taxation on BBC radio and television.

A chartered accountant by training, Carl began his professional life in 1983, in the Birmingham office of one of the 'Big 4' accountancy firms. He qualified as a double prize-winner and immediately began specialising in taxation.

After 17 years honing his skills with major firms, Carl began the new millennium in January 2000 by launching his own Edinburgh-based tax consultancy practice, Bayley Consulting, through which he now provides advice on a wide variety of UK taxation issues, especially property taxation, Inheritance Tax planning and matters affecting small and medium-sized businesses.

As well as being Taxcafe.co.uk's Senior Consultant, Carl is also Chairman of the Institute Members in Scotland group and a member of the governing Council of the Institute of Chartered Accountants in England and Wales.

When he isn't working, Carl takes on the equally taxing challenges of hill walking and writing poetry.

Dedication

As usual, this book is dedicated to the two very special ladies who have shaped my life:
To Isabel, whose unflinching support has seen me through the best and the worst.
And to Diana, who made it all possible.

Thanks

Sincere thanks are also due to my good friend and colleague, Nick, who believed in me long before I did.

C.B., Edinburgh, April 2004

Contents

Appendices

Chapter 1

Introduction to Inheritance Tax

Generally speaking, I find that the oldest sayings are the truest. One old saying is "There are only two certainties in life: Death and Taxes".

The place where these two great "certainties" meet is "Inheritance Tax", and it is through the medium of this tax that the Inland Revenue will aim to get their final pound of flesh from you, just as you have departed this life.

Most people spend their lifetime trying to accumulate a reasonable amount of wealth, to take care of themselves in their old age and then to pass on any remaining surplus to their children. Much of the Government's fiscal policy is aimed at encouraging this type of behaviour.

It is somewhat unfair then, that without careful planning and a great deal of pre-emptive action, most families will ultimately face a huge Inheritance Tax bill.

Unchecked, this tax bill will rob your family of a significant proportion of their rightful inheritance – up to 40% of it, in fact.

Many people are absolutely appalled at this prospect which, of course, is where Inheritance Tax planning comes in!

Some years ago, the Labour Party accused the then Conservative Government of allowing Inheritance Tax to become a "voluntary tax", paid only by the unwary, ill-advised and unprepared taxpayer, whilst wealthier taxpayers took good (but expensive) professional advice and avoided the tax.

Certainly, there was an element of truth in this accusation. Furthermore, it remained equally true for almost seven years since, despite fears to the contrary, "New Labour" initially did little to change the situation after coming to power in 1997.

However, on 10th December 2003, it became quite clear that the 'phoney war' was over, as Chancellor of the Exchequer, Gordon Brown announced plans for a new Income Tax benefit-in-kind charge which will hit many families attempting to plan for the inevitable.

With or without the proposed new Income Tax charge, what remains true to this day is the fact that it is the moderately wealthy members of society who suffer the greatest proportionate burden of Inheritance Tax when compared to their overall wealth.

In my experience, Inheritance Tax tends to be a tax which is predominantly paid by the moderately wealthy citizens of middle England (as well as middle Scotland, Wales and Northern Ireland too).

The problem for many people in the middle wealth bracket is that they face a fundamental dichotomy.

On the one hand they have, on paper, sufficient wealth to leave their family with a very substantial tax burden when they pass away.

On the other hand, however, they do not really have a great deal of disposable income, despite leading reasonably modest lifestyles.

This means that the very simple expedient of simply giving all of their wealth away is, in practical terms, simply not an option.

Recent trends have added to this problem. The rapid increase in property values over the last decade has pushed more and more people into the Inheritance Tax bracket, especially in the "hotspots" like London and the South East and other desirable areas, such as my home town, Edinburgh.

The second factor adding impetus to the "asset rich/cash poor" situation, which many people now find themselves in, is the current low level of interest rates, coupled with very disappointing returns on the stock market.

In short, what this means is that a lot of capital produces only a modest income, leaving a great many people, with very little real wealth today, serious Inheritance Tax problems for tomorrow!

Yet there still remain two effective ways to avoid Inheritance Tax:

- Die poor, or

- Plan ahead

Most of us find the first option somewhat unpalatable, and also quite difficult to achieve without a remarkable sense of timing!

Until recently, "planning ahead" has also been seen as the prerogative of the very wealthiest members of society, leaving the moderately wealthy to pick up the bill!

However, my aim in this guide is to help put an end to this situation.

If the Government is still, to some extent, prepared to allow Inheritance Tax to be "voluntary" then why should anyone volunteer?

Early and careful planning is the key to reducing the eventual Inheritance Tax burden on your family and you don't need to be a millionaire to do it (or to <u>need</u> to do it either, for that matter!).

Besides which, a great many people are surprised to discover that, when they do add up all of their assets, they are, in fact, millionaires anyway (on paper, at least).

Whilst some tax can still be saved through "last-minute" planning, a great deal more unnecessary tax can be avoided by planning for death and taxes throughout your lifetime. Read on and I will show you how.

Chapter 2

A Brief History of Inheritance Tax

Inheritance Tax, as we know it today, arrived in 1984, the brainchild of Margaret Thatcher and her then loyal Chancellor, Geoffrey Howe. 'IHT', as the tax would become known to those of us who were young accountancy students at the time, was little more than a re-branding of its predecessor, Capital Transfer Tax (fondly known as 'CTT').

Capital Transfer Tax, in turn, had replaced the earlier and rather more draconian Estate Duty, which had, in its day, played a major part in turning many of Britain's stately homes into amusement parks! It is quite ironic that Inheritance Tax should have such a long lineage because it is, of course, one's descendants who will suffer its effects.

The principal difference between Inheritance Tax and its predecessors is the fact that there is a general exemption for most lifetime transfers (see further in Chapter 10 below).

This is part of the reason behind the accusations that it is a voluntary tax, since simply giving all of one's wealth away would initially seem to be an easy way to escape the tax altogether. However, inevitably, as we will see later in this guide, Inheritance Tax is not quite that easy to avoid. You have to survive for at least seven years after leaving yourself completely destitute (and homeless), for a start.

Chapter 3

Why Worry About Inheritance Tax?

Of course **you** won't actually have to pay any Inheritance Tax on your own estate. Furthermore, for most people, everything can safely be left to their widow or widower free from any Inheritance Tax (see further in Chapter 9 below).

And, if you have no other dependants or potential beneficiaries to care about, but simply resent paying any unnecessary tax, you can simply leave it all to charity (see Chapter 14).

But most people _do_ have someone they care about. Usually they have children or other family or friends whom they want to see benefit from the assets they have built up in their lifetime and they don't want to see the Government taking 40% of it away.

Even if, in the first instance, you are leaving everything tax free to your surviving spouse, your accumulated wealth will eventually be hit by Inheritance Tax if you don't plan ahead. As we will see later in the guide, you need to take action **now** in order to safeguard your family's future prosperity.

Alternatively, you may be in the position of being the potential beneficiary yourself, trying to get an elderly relative to plan for the preservation of _your_ inheritance.

Either way, there is plenty to worry about!

But Am I Wealthy Enough to Need to Worry?

Most people are quite surprised to discover just how much they are actually worth. How often have you heard someone say "I'm worth more dead than alive". Very often, especially as we get older, it's true. (In pure financial terms only, of course.)

This is basically because it takes an enormous amount of capital just to support one person. When that person dies, the capital which was previously tied up in supporting them is freed. (After the Government get its share of it, that is!)

Hence, although you may not feel particularly wealthy, you may still find that you have a large potential Inheritance Tax bill.

You'd be amazed at just how many "paper millionaires" there are these days. Take a look at this example:

Example
Rosemary, a widow, owns a large detached house, which her late husband left to her. The house is bigger than she really needs, but it was the former marital home, so she is quite attached to it. She has been advised that its current market value is £450,000.

Rosemary is retired and lives off her savings and an investment portfolio which was also left to her by her late husband. Although these produce an income of only £16,000 per annum, their total value is approximately £425,000.

Whilst they were married, Rosemary and her husband enjoyed collecting paintings. She recently had their modest collection valued and was astounded to discover that it is now worth £80,000.

Rosemary also has some jewellery, some silver and a few antiques. Altogether, these are worth £40,000. Lastly, she has a small car, worth £5,000.

Nobody would call Rosemary rich by any stretch of the imagination. She's living off only £16,000 a year. But add it all up and you will find that she is a millionaire!

This means that Rosemary's family has a potential Inheritance Tax bill of £294,800!

And you don't need to be anywhere near as "wealthy" as Rosemary to have an Inheritance Tax problem. Once your estate is worth over £263,000, you have a potential exposure to tax at 40% on the excess.

£263,000! What's that these days? A flat, a car and a few savings and you're there!

So, yes, generally speaking, if you can afford to buy this guide, you probably are wealthy enough to need to worry about Inheritance Tax!

Chapter 4

Where Does the Tax Come From?

The statistics on the main sources of Inheritance Tax make interesting reading:

- 41% comes from *people's own homes!*

- 26% comes from cash (including savings accounts, deposit accounts, etc.).

- 12% comes from quoted shares and securities.

- The remaining balance comes from household personal effects, insurance proceeds and other land holdings.

The top item on the list is the family home, which means that this tax is not, as many people would like to think, predominantly raised on the rich.

Inheritance Tax is mainly derived from the estates of normal people whose only "crime" is to have simply been careful with their finances all their life.

We will return to the subject of Inheritance Tax on the family home later in the guide (see Chapter 20).

Wealth Warning

Household personal effects are generally overvalued,
resulting in unnecessary overpayments of Inheritance
Tax. The valuations which most people have on their
personal effects (jewellery, antiques, silverware, etc,)
tend to be insurance valuations. However, the amount on
which Inheritance Tax is payable should only be the open
market value of the assets and this is often considerably
less.

Chapter 5

Who Pays Inheritance Tax?

For UK domiciled individuals, Inheritance Tax arises on:

- The whole value of their entire estate at the time of their death, wherever situated, less:

  i) The "Nil Rate Band" (£263,000 for deaths on or after 6th April 2004).
  ii) Any other exemptions & reliefs (see Chapter 14).

  and

- Certain lifetime gifts and other transfers (see Chapter 10).

Before those of you born in a sunnier climate start to rejoice, you should note that you will also be deemed to be UK domiciled for Inheritance Tax purposes, and taxed accordingly, if you have been Tax Resident here for at least 17 out of the last 20 UK tax years (years ended 5th April).

Note that this does not affect your position in respect of Income Tax or Capital Gains Tax. For this reason, it is usually worth retaining foreign Domicile, even if you have deemed UK Domicile for Inheritance Tax purposes.

If you are neither UK Domiciled, nor deemed to be UK Domiciled, as explained above, then Inheritance Tax will generally only arise on any UK assets which you hold, including land and buildings situated within the UK.

Again, this liability arises on death or in the event of certain lifetime gifts, which we will cover later in the guide.

A few countries (see Appendix B) have Double Tax Treaties with the UK which may affect your position if you are Domiciled there. This also applies to the question of "deemed domicile".

What Does "Domiciled" Mean?

Broadly speaking, "Domicile" is a concept similar to nationality and, for most people, it will be pretty obvious where they are domiciled.

Nevertheless, "Domicile" does not entirely correspond to nationality, and can sometimes be a highly complex matter.

For a detailed examination of Domicile, refer to Chapter 26 at the end of this guide.

But Who Actually <u>Pays</u> the Tax?

1. Death

Most Inheritance Tax arises on death and, of course, the deceased is not around to pick up the bill!

The liability for Inheritance Tax arising on death will generally fall on the deceased's Personal Representatives (who must settle it out of the assets of the estate).

There are, however, some exceptions to this general rule, as follows:

i) Where specific property vests in a beneficiary (e.g. "I leave my house to my sister Julie").

ii) Where a beneficiary becomes entitled to a life interest in property under the terms of the Will.

iii) Where a bequest is made on the specific condition that the beneficiary meets the Inheritance Tax arising out of their legacy.

iv) Where property is already held in Trust (as explained in Chapter 17).

In cases under (i), (ii) and (iii) above, it is the beneficiaries themselves who must bear the tax.

However, where specific bequests are being made (as in (i) above), it is possible to draw up your Will in such a way that the Inheritance Tax falls on your Personal Representatives (to be settled out of the general assets of your estate).

For property already held in trust, as in (iv) above, the Inheritance Tax may fall on the trustees or on a beneficiary of that trust, depending on the exact circumstances.

"Grossing Up"

The amount of Inheritance Tax payable on a specific asset or bequest may be affected by whether or not it is paid by the Personal Representatives.

This is due to the procedure known as "Grossing Up" and is best explained by way of a short example.

Example

John leaves his eldest son Paul a house worth £90,000, on condition that he settles any tax arising. He also leaves his younger son George the sum of £90,000 in cash, stating in his Will that this sum should be free of all taxes and other encumbrances.

As Paul has to settle the Inheritance Tax on his bequest directly, he will pay Inheritance Tax at a straightforward rate of 40%, i.e. £36,000.

The Inheritance Tax on George's bequest will, however, be paid by John's Personal Representatives, Ringo & Co. This brings into play the procedure known as "Grossing Up".

In other words, George's bequest must be grossed up to account for the Inheritance Tax being paid out of John's estate.

The "Grossing Up" factor is 2/3rds. Hence, an additional two thirds must be added to George's bequest of £90,000, producing a grossed up amount of £150,000 (£90,000 PLUS two thirds of £90,000, i.e. £60,000).

The Inheritance Tax due on this bequest is therefore £60,000 (i.e. £150,000 x 40%).

As can readily be seen, this is equal to the amount of the "Grossing Up", meaning that Ringo & Co. can now give the original sum of £90,000 to George free of any further tax liabilities.

(**NOTE:** In this example, for the sake of simplicity, I have ignored the impact of any applicable reliefs and exemptions, including the Nil Rate Band. I have also assumed that there are sufficient other assets within the estate to enable the Personal Representatives to settle the Inheritance Tax liability arising from George's bequest.)

"Grossing Up" becomes very important when, as in the Example above, a number of different beneficiaries are involved.

However, in the simple case of a single beneficiary, it has no effect since the same total amount of Inheritance Tax will always be payable out of the estate.

The impact of "Grossing Up" is simply to decide how much Inheritance Tax is borne by each beneficiary. Someone will always be entitled to the residuary amount left in the estate after dealing with all of the specific bequests and it is that person who will ultimately suffer the impact of the "Grossing Up" calculations.

2. Lifetime Transfers

The primary responsibility for any Inheritance Tax arising on lifetime transfers falls on transferors themselves. It is possible, however, to stipulate that the transferee should bear any Inheritance Tax arising.

Additional Inheritance Tax liabilities frequently arise when the transferor dies within seven years of a lifetime transfer. These liabilities usually fall on the transferee.

"Grossing Up" can also apply to lifetime transfers.

Inheritance Tax on lifetime transfers is examined in detail in Chapter 10 below.

Chapter 6

The Basic Calculation on Death

On death, Inheritance Tax is levied, generally at one single rate of 40%, on the entire value of your estate, less certain exemptions. The most important exemptions are the Nil Rate Band, which is £263,000 for deaths occurring on or after 6th April 2004, and the exemption for transfers to spouses (see Chapter 9).

What is Your Estate?

Your "estate" means everything you own, including land and property, shares and securities, savings accounts, cash, antiques, jewellery, paintings, your car, your furniture and anything else which has any value whatsoever.

Certain other items must also be brought into your estate for Inheritance Tax purposes, including any life interests you have in trusts (Chapter 17) and any non-exempt gifts you made in the seven years prior to your death (Chapter 12). (Reduced Inheritance Tax rates do, however, apply to gifts made between three and seven years prior to death.)

Any liabilities you have will be deducted, such as your mortgage, overdrafts, bank loans, credit card bills, amounts borrowed from friends or family (if these can be proven) and any outstanding utility bills. You may even deduct outstanding Income Tax and

Capital Gains Tax liabilities!

"Reasonable" funeral expenses may also be deducted. What is "reasonable" depends on your standard of living. (In one extreme case, the expense of a private army providing an honour guard at the funeral was deemed to be "reasonable".)

In other words, subject to a few technical adjustments, your "estate" is basically your total net worth.

All of the property transferred on your death is subject to Inheritance Tax in the same way, whether it transfers under the terms of your Will, by intestacy, by survivorship (for jointly held property) or by any other means.

Tax Tip

Many people take out insurance policies to cover outstanding liabilities, such as credit card bills or bank loans, if they should pass away unexpectedly. The result of this is that these liabilities would not be deductible from the value of the estate as they were automatically settled on the taxpayer's death.

It would be far better to make provision for such liabilities by other means (see Chapter 19) and thus ensure that they are deducted from the value of your estate for Inheritance Tax purposes.

Wealth Warning

Many people assume that tax-advantaged products, such as Individual Savings Accounts ("ISAs") and Personal Equity Plans ("PEPs") are exempt from Inheritance Tax because they are supposedly "tax-free".

Unfortunately, this is not the case and **ALL** assets have to be included in your estate, regardless of their treatment for Income Tax or Capital Gains Tax purposes.

To illustrate the basic Inheritance Tax calculation, let's take a look at a very simple example:

Example

Arthur has been very careful with his money all his life. At the time of his death in December 2004, his estate amounts to £2,000,000.

Arthur's Will leaves his entire estate to his son Tony, so there are no exemptions available, other than the Nil Rate Band.

The first £263,000 of Arthur's estate is exempt from Inheritance Tax, as it is covered by the Nil Rate Band (Chapter 8). The remaining £1,737,000, however, is charged to Inheritance Tax at 40%, giving rise to a tax charge of £694,800!

Note that "Grossing Up" does not apply in the above example, as Tony will bear all of the Inheritance Tax arising.

Chapter 7

Payment & Administration

7.1 Payment

Inheritance Tax arising on death is normally due six months after the end of the month of death. Hence, in Arthur's case (see Example above), it will be due by 1st July 2005. Personal Representatives may sometimes have to pay the tax even earlier however, as the liability is triggered when they deliver their accounts for probate purposes.

One slight consolation though is that when the tax arising is based on the value of land or buildings within the deceased's estate, the Personal Representatives may instead elect for it to be paid in ten equal yearly instalments, commencing six months after the month of death. If the property concerned is subsequently sold, however, then all of the remaining Inheritance Tax relating to that property, (which has not yet been paid under the instalment system), becomes payable immediately.

Interest is charged on, and added to, payments made by instalments.

Interest is, of course, also charged on late payments under any other circumstances.

The current interest rate applying to both instalments and other late payments is 4% (one of the best interest rates in the tax system, it must be said).

7.2 Accounts

The Personal Representatives of any estate which is large enough to give rise to an Inheritance Tax liability, or of certain other larger estates (as defined in Government Regulations), must deliver a set of accounts to the Inland Revenue detailing:

- The assets of the estate and their value at the time of the deceased's death,
- Lifetime transfers made by the deceased within the seven years prior to death,
- Any relevant reliefs and exemptions claimed, and
- The amount of Inheritance Tax due.

The Personal Representatives of some smaller estates (i.e. those with a total value well within the nil rate band) are usually exempted from the requirement to produce detailed accounts to the Inland Revenue, although they must, of course, still provide some limited information to the Probate Service or the Scottish Court Service, as the case may be.

However, the Inland Revenue monitor this process via information provided to them by the Probate Service or its Scottish counterpart. In some cases, they will call for a full set of accounts from these smaller estates as a 'check'.

Proposals announced on 17th March 2004 should hopefully reduce the administrative burden on such small estates, as the Inland Revenue will, in future, be able to obtain accounts directly from the Probate Service or the Scottish Court Service, meaning that the Personal Representatives of such small estates need only deal with the Government once. (I should think so too!)

This very sensible change should come into force in late 2004.

7.3 Penalties

Further proposals included in the 2004 Budget mean that a new Inheritance Tax penalty regime is to be introduced after the 2004 Finance Act becomes law. (Any Act of Parliament only becomes law when it obtains 'Royal Assent', which, in this case, is expected to take place in June or July 2004.)

Under this new regime, penalties will be imposed as follows:

- Up to £3,000 for failure to submit an Inheritance Tax account within 12 months of the due date (see section 7.1 above).

- Up to £3,000 for failure to notify the Inland Revenue of the variation of a disposition on death within 12 months of when such a notification is due (see Chapter 25).

- £100 for late delivery of an Inheritance Tax account, unless the amount of tax involved is less than £100, or there is a reasonable excuse for the late delivery of the account.

It is claimed that these new penalties are meant to bring the Inheritance Tax regime more in line with the penalty rules for Income Tax and Capital Gains Tax. Funnily, enough though, one of the very few 'reasonable excuses' which the Inland Revenue will usually accept for a late Income Tax Self Assessment Return is death. Surely then, as far as Inheritance Tax is concerned, everyone must have a 'reasonable excuse' for late delivery of accounts?

Sadly, in reality, I don't suppose that the Inland Revenue will see it that way. However, considering the circumstances under which Inheritance Tax arises, I really have to say that the imposition of penalties does amount to 'kicking people when they're down'!

At the same time, there will be a relaxation for the existing penalties applying to the submission of 'negligent or fraudulent' material to the Inland Revenue. After Royal Assent, penalties will no longer be imposed in cases where the negligence or fraud did not actually result in any change to the amount of Inheritance Tax due.

Now, in the case of negligence, I can accept this as a sensible relaxation. Why, oh why, however, is the Government proposing to exempt the fraudulent? Against a background of ever-tightening regulation under anti-Money Laundering regulations and the Proceeds of Crime Act, this hardly makes any sense!

Chapter 8

The Nil Rate Band

The Nil Rate Band is perhaps the most important Inheritance Tax exemption for the vast majority of people. As the name suggests, what the Nil Rate Band means is that an Inheritance Tax rate of nil is applied to the first part of your estate, which falls within this band.

The amount of Nil Rate Band available depends on the date of death. More accurately, it depends on the UK tax year of death.

Like many other tax exemptions, the Nil Rate Band is generally increased, on an annual basis, in line with inflation. However, as is also the case with many other tax exemptions, the increase is only given by reference to retail price inflation.

When "New Labour" came to power in 1997, the Nil Rate Band stood at £215,000. In the seven year period since then, it has been increased by a total of 22.3%, to £263,000. However, in the six-year period from 1997 to 2003, house prices rose by an average of 84% nationally (115% in London). Hence, if the Nil Rate Band had been increased, as seems more appropriate, in line with house price inflation, rather than retail price inflation, it should have stood at £395,000 by 2003 (or £462,000 if it had a London "weighting").

Given these dramatic recent increases in property values, plus the general increase in the levels of personal wealth in the UK, what this actually means is that the Government's "take" from

Inheritance Tax is steadily increasing.

In his Budget statement on 17th March 2004, Chancellor Gordon Brown announced that the latest increase in the Nil Rate Band would "exempt 95% of all estates from this tax".

What he is referring to there, of course, is <u>current</u> deaths. When one considers the potential Inheritance Tax liabilities of people who are still working, or in the early years of their retirement, the story is very different!

In fact, the current annual take from the tax of £3 billion is forecast to increase to a level of **£8 billion a year** in the near future.

The Nil Rate Band applying in recent years has been as follows:

For deaths occurring:

On or after 6th April 2004:	£263,000
Between 6th April 2003 and 5th April 2004:	£255,000
Between 6th April 2002 and 5th April 2003:	£250,000
Between 6th April 2001 and 5th April 2002:	£242,000
Between 6th April 2000 and 5th April 2001:	£234,000

It is important to note that each individual has their own Nil Rate Band. I will come back to this point, and explain its significance in Inheritance Tax planning, later.

Chapter 9

Transfers to Spouses

Except as noted below, all transfers of property to your spouse are completely exempt from Inheritance Tax. This covers both lifetime transfers and transfers made on death.

Exception – Spouses with Separate Domicile

Where one of you is UK Domiciled and the other is not, the general exemption for transfers between spouses is restricted.

In this case, only the first £55,000 of transfers from the UK Domiciled spouse to the foreign Domiciled spouse is exempt. (There is no restriction on transfers in the opposite direction – why would there be? - such transfers would potentially increase the Inland Revenue's tax haul. They might also have foreign tax implications!)

Other Exceptions

The general exemption for transfers between spouses is also restricted in a few other circumstances. The exemption may be lost where:

i) The transfer to the spouse only takes effect after the expiry of another third party's interest in the asset or after the expiry of some other period of time. (**Tax Tip:** It is, however, acceptable to have a condition in your Will that your spouse must survive you by a certain period before becoming entitled to the asset.)

ii) The transfer is dependent on a condition and that condition is not satisfied within twelve months after the date of transfer.

iii) The transfer is only made as consideration for the transfer of a reversionary interest in some other property.

iv) The transfer is made into a trust, where the transferee spouse has an 'interest in possession' (see Chapter 17) which comes to an end before the death of the donor spouse.

For those of you who follow such things, exception (iv) was introduced with effect from 20th June 2003 to block a previously popular avoidance scheme which became the subject of the 'Eversden' case.

What is a Spouse?

Sounds like a daft question, doesn't it? Well, it's not – read on.

For Inheritance Tax purposes, a spouse must be your legally married husband or wife.

Although not specifically mentioned in the legislation, it would seem likely that a person ceases to be your spouse if you are legally separated from them or separated form them in circumstances which are likely to become permanent.

Wealth Warning

The exemption applies only to legally married couples. There is no Inheritance Tax exemption for transfers to common-law partners!

Tax Tip

If you intend leaving most of your estate to a common-law partner then, if you can, try to get married before you die. Deathbed marriages have been known to save **millions** of pounds in Inheritance Tax and it is one planning device which is almost impossible for the Inland Revenue to overturn.

Chapter 10

Lifetime Transfers

In theory, Inheritance Tax is chargeable on any "transfer of value" made by any person at any time. The reason we tend to think of it as mainly applying on death is the fact that most lifetime transfers are exempt, or at least only become chargeable in the event of death within seven years.

What is a "Transfer of Value"?

A transfer of value occurs whenever you dispose of something and, as a result, the value of your estate is reduced.

This does not apply to any "transactions at arm's length" between unconnected persons, so that merely striking a "poor bargain" would not be a transfer of value.

Example

John buys a car for £5,000 from Alexei, a second-hand car dealer. It turns out, however, that the car is an absolute wreck, worth at best around £800!

Poor John. However, at least there is no "transfer of value" here, since John and Alexei are not connected.

If, on the other hand, John had bought the car from his sister, Janet, there would have been a transfer of value, as they are "connected persons" (see Appendix D).

Nevertheless, a transaction with a connected person will not give rise to any transfer of value, as long as it is carried out in the same way as it would have been if it had been an arm's length transaction with an unconnected person.

Example

Mick wants to buy his father's house. His father, Keith, obtains an independent valuation on the house, which indicates that it is worth £200,000. He therefore sells the house to Mick for this amount.

Unbeknown to Mick, Keith and the independent valuer, plans for a new bypass are just about to be announced, as a result of which the house's value will increase dramatically.

This may look like a "transfer of value" but it isn't because Mick and Keith have struck the same bargain as would have been struck between unconnected persons.

The Amount of the "Transfer of Value"

As stated above, a "transfer of value" occurs when you make a disposal which is not at arm's length and, as a result, there is a reduction in the total value of your estate.

The simplest type of "transfer of value" is therefore a straightforward gift. If you give someone £10,000 in cash that is a "transfer of value" of £10,000, if you give someone a painting worth £5,000, that is a "transfer of value" of £5,000.

A "transfer of value" also occurs, however, when sales take place between connected persons at an undervalue or at an overvalue.

If you sell your son a painting, which is worth £10,000, for only

£2,000, that is a "transfer of value" of £8,000. If you buy a car, which is worth only £1,000, from your daughter and pay her £5,000, that is a "transfer of value" of £4,000.

But what is important to remember is that it is the reduction in the value of your overall estate which gives rise to the "transfer of value".

Example

Bjorn has a set of six antique chairs, worth £20,000. He gives his son Benny one of the chairs. The value of this single chair, or any other chair which is not part of a complete set, is only £1,500.

However, the "transfer of value" here is not the value of Benny's single chair, £1,500.

No, the "transfer of value" is the reduction in the value of Bjorn's overall estate. Previously, he had a set of chairs worth £20,000. After the gift to Benny, he has five chairs worth £1,500 each, a total of £7,500.

Hence, the reduction in the value of Bjorn's estate, and thus the amount of the "transfer of value", is £12,500.

Inheritance Tax on Lifetime Transfers

Having established how to calculate the amount of any lifetime transfer for Inheritance Tax purposes, it must now be admitted that very few of them actually give rise to any Inheritance Tax in the first instance.

However, it remains important to realise that lifetime transfers are all potentially chargeable to Inheritance Tax.

The reason for this seemingly contradictory position is that any lifetime transfers to another individual, or to some types of trust, which are not otherwise exempted, are treated as "Potentially Exempt Transfers". These are covered in detail in Chapter 11 below.

The major exceptions to this, though, are transfers to:
- Discretionary Trusts, or
- Companies

Such transfers may be immediately chargeable to Inheritance Tax. These transfers are therefore referred to as "chargeable transfers".

Transfers of value into companies are rare and the major incidence of chargeable lifetime transfers are therefore transfers into Discretionary Trusts. These trusts are a major Inheritance Tax planning tool and are covered in detail in Chapter 21.

The amount of the chargeable transfer is arrived at by deducting any available exemptions (see Chapter 13 below) from the "transfer of value".

The amount of Inheritance Tax due is then calculated as follows:

Other chargeable transfers within the last seven years	X
PLUS	
This chargeable transfer	X
LESS	
Nil Rate Band	(X)

EQUALS the amount on which Inheritance Tax is now chargeable.

Inheritance Tax on lifetime transfers is charged at half death rates, i.e. 20%.

Example
In this example, we are ignoring all exemptions and reliefs, other than the Nil Rate Band.

Two years ago, Elvis gifted some investments worth £50,000 into a Discretionary Trust, thus giving rise to a Chargeable Transfer. No Inheritance Tax was payable at the time, of course, as this was well within his Nil Rate Band.

Elvis now gifts his former home, Graceland, which is worth £350,000, into a Discretionary Trust (for the purposes of this example, it does not matter whether this is the same trust or not), on condition that the trust settles any Inheritance Tax arising.

The trust's Inheritance Tax liability is calculated as follows:

Previous Chargeable Transfers within last 7 years:	£50,000
ADD	
This Chargeable Transfer	£350,000
EQUALS:	
Cumulative Chargeable Transfers	£400,000
LESS:	
Nil Rate Band	£263,000
EQUALS:	
Amount chargeable	£137,000
Inheritance Tax Payable at lifetime rate (20%)	£27,400

Alternative Scenario – with 'Grossing Up'

Note that, if Elvis had settled the Inheritance Tax himself, it would have been subject to "Grossing Up", as follows:

Amount chargeable, as before	*£137,000*
Grossing Up factor – ¼	*£34,250*
Grossed Up Amount	*£171,250*
Inheritance Tax Payable at lifetime rate (20%)	*£34,250*

Wealth Warning

Note that, in this example, Graceland was Elvis' <u>former</u> home. This is a very important point since, as we will see later in the guide, it is very difficult to make an Inheritance Tax-effective transfer of your current home.

Tax Tip

If Elvis was married, he could have avoided any Inheritance Tax on his gift of Graceland by first transferring it into joint names with his wife before they both jointly gifted it to the Discretionary Trust. Each of them would then have made a Chargeable Transfer of only £175,000. Even after taking his previous Chargeable Transfer into account, Elvis would then have been covered by his Nil Rate Band.

(Elvis' wife would also be covered by her Nil Rate Band as long as she had not made other Chargeable Transfers within the last seven years in excess of £88,000.)

Avoiding "Grossing Up"

In the above example, we have looked at the situation where the Inheritance Tax is paid by the transferee (the Trust), as well as the situation where it is paid by the transferor (Elvis himself).

More tax is generally payable where the transferor is settling the liability. This is because the transferor is deemed to be making a gift not only of the original asset transferred, but also of the tax arising. This is because the "transfer of value" is once again calculated by reference to the reduction in value of the transferor's overall estate and the payment of the Inheritance Tax arising naturally increases the amount of that reduction.

The bad news here is that, in the absence of any evidence to the contrary, the transferor is always assumed to be liable for any

Inheritance Tax. Hence, if care is not exercised, you may find that the value of any gifts which you make turns out to be 25% larger than you had expected!

The way to avoid this is to draw up a memorandum of your gift which stipulates that the transferee is to pay any Inheritance Tax arising. An example of a suitable memorandum is included as item 2 in Appendix E.

Chapter 11

Potentially Exempt Transfers

As explained in the previous chapter, most lifetime transfers are either fully exempt (see Chapter 13) or they are Potentially Exempt Transfers (or "PETs", for short).

Any lifetime transfers to any of the following, which are not otherwise exempt, will be Potentially Exempt Transfers:

- Another individual (except as noted below)
- An Interest In Possession Trust*
- An Accumulation and Maintenance Trust*
- A Disabled Trust*

* - See Chapter 17 for an explanation of Trust terminology.

Exceptions

The following transfers to other individuals will not be Potentially Exempt Transfers:

- Any transfers to your UK-Domiciled spouse (these are fully exempt, except as noted in Chapter 9 above).

- The first £55,000 of transfers to your non-UK Domiciled spouse (again, these are fully exempt except as noted in Chapter 9).

So What Do We Mean By "Potentially Exempt"?

Put simply, these transfers are <u>potentially</u> exempt because all the transferor has to do is to survive for seven years after making the transfer for it to then become fully exempt and completely free and clear of any possible Inheritance Tax liability (subject to the Gifts with Reservation rules – see Chapter 16).

Example

On 11th August 1997 Chuck gave £1,000,000 to his little brother Richard.

Sadly, on 12th August 2004, Chuck is electrocuted whilst playing his electric guitar in a rainstorm.

The gift to Richard was a Potentially Exempt Transfer and, since Chuck survived the requisite seven years, this sum is completely exempt from Inheritance Tax on Chuck's death.

Tax Tip

If Chuck had died just one day earlier, Inheritance Tax would have been payable on his gift to Richard (see further in Chapter 12 below). Hence, it is essential to have the documentary evidence to prove that the gift took place when it did. A memorandum along the lines of either item 1 or item 2 (as appropriate) in Appendix E would suffice for this purpose.

Chapter 12

Death Within 7 Years of a Lifetime Transfer

For Capital Gains Tax purposes, death is often a very good tax planning strategy. The same cannot be said, however, of Inheritance Tax.

Both Chargeable Transfers and Potentially Exempt Transfers made in the seven year period prior to death are brought back into the deceased's estate for Inheritance Tax purposes.

This applies whether any Inheritance Tax was actually payable at the time of the transfer or not.

As a result of this, additional Inheritance Tax liabilities may arise and these are the responsibility of the transferees. In other words, the situation may be like this:

> "I'm very sorry to hear about your father, son, but do you remember that gift of £10,000 he gave you two years ago? Well, I'm afraid you're going to have to pay some tax on it now."

Subject to the Tapering provisions (see below), Inheritance Tax now becomes payable at the death rate (40%) on these transfers. Any Inheritance Tax paid on the original transfer, however, may be deducted, so that it is just the excess which arises on death.

Tapering

Fortunately, there is some relief where death occurs more than three, but less than seven, years after the transfer. In these cases, the rate of Inheritance Tax arising on the death is tapered as follows:

No. of years after transfer which Death occurs:	Proportion of "Death Rate" Payable
Not more than 3	100% (=IHT @ 40%)
More than 3 but not more than 4	80% (=IHT @ 32%)
More than 4 but not more than 5	60% (=IHT @ 24%)
More than 5 but not more than 6	40% (=IHT @ 16%)
More than 6 but not more than 7	20% (=IHT @ 8%)

Where the transferee is a trust, the trustees may also claim a reduction in their Inheritance Tax liability if the value of the asset transferred to them has fallen by the time of the transferor's death.

In this case, the transferee's Inheritance Tax liability is based on the value of the gifted asset at the date of death.

This is not an absolute saving of Inheritance Tax however, as the transferor's Personal Representatives remain liable for the balance.

Tax Tip

Thanks to the tapering provisions, Inheritance Tax starts to be saved once the transferor manages to survive just three years. Hence, even if you don't think that Great Aunt Maude stands any chance of lasting seven years, it's still worth looking at getting her to make some gifts.

Wealth Warning

Note that the reductions in the amount of Inheritance Tax payable occur on the **day after** the anniversaries of the gift, not the anniversary itself!

In the case of Chargeable Lifetime Transfers (see Chapter 10 above), the tapering provisions could result in the final Inheritance Tax liability on death actually being less than the amount already paid.

Unfortunately, this simply means that no further Inheritance Tax is due; it does not result in any repayment.

The effect of all this is best illustrated by way of an example.

Example

(As in previous examples, we will ignore any exemptions and reliefs, other than the Nil Rate Band.)

Roy, a kind, generous and rich old man, dies on 3rd December 2004. In the last few years of his life, he made the following gifts:

- *On 13th January 1998, he gave £300,000 in cash to the Wilbury Discretionary Trust. He paid £19,250 in Inheritance Tax at that time (Grossing up applied).*

- *On 8th May 2000, he gave Bob £100,000 in cash.*

- *On 3rd December 2001, he gave Tom some shares in Heartbreaker.com plc, which were worth £80,000 at that time, but only worth £1,000 at the time of Roy's death.*

- *On 30th August 2002, he transferred some shares in the Electric Light Company inc. into Jeff's Life Interest Trust. At that time, these were worth £50,000 but, by the time of Roy's death, they were worth only £30,000.*

The Inheritance Tax payable on Roy's death by each of these transferees is as follows:

The Wilbury Discretionary Trust

Due to the grossing up provisions, this is deemed to have been a gift of £319,250. As this gift was within the last seven years of Roy's life, it is pulled back into his estate for the purposes of his Inheritance Tax calculation.

It is worth noting, therefore, that the Nil Rate Band is already used up on this single gift. (The Nil Rate Band is used against this gift as it is the oldest item being brought into account.

Transfers are always dealt with in chronological order for Inheritance Tax purposes.)

After deducting the Nil Rate Band of £263,000 from the deemed gift of £319,250, there remains a chargeable sum of £56,250.

As the gift took place more than six, but less than seven, years before Roy's death, Inheritance Tax is chargeable at only 20% of the death rate, i.e. 8%.

Hence the Inheritance Tax charge on this gift arising on Roy's death is £5,140. As this is less than the Inheritance Tax already paid by Roy on the lifetime transfer (£19,250), no further Inheritance Tax is therefore payable.

Bob

The gift to Bob took place more than four, but less than five, years before Roy's death. Inheritance Tax is therefore chargeable at 60% of the death rate, i.e. 24%.

Bob therefore has an Inheritance Tax liability of £24,000.

Tom

Tom really is going to be heartbroken. His gift took place exactly three years before Roy's death.

Unfortunately, Inheritance Tax tapering only begins on the day **after** the third anniversary of the gift.

Inheritance Tax is therefore payable at the full death rate, 40%. Furthermore, Tom is not entitled to claim any reduction in his liability, as the gift was made to him personally and not as the beneficiary of a Trust.

Tom is therefore left with some shares which are virtually worthless and an Inheritance Tax liability of £32,000 (40% x £80,000).

Sometimes it **does** pay to look a gift horse in the mouth!

Jeff's Life Interest Trust

This gift took place within the last three years of Roy's life, so there is no tapering of the Inheritance Tax liability.

The full liability is therefore £20,000 (40% x £50,000).

However, the trustees of Jeff's Life Interest Trust may claim to reduce their Inheritance Tax liability in line with the value of the gifted shares at the time of Roy's death, i.e. £30,000. This would reduce their Inheritance Tax liability to only £12,000 (40% x £30,000). The balance of £8,000 would be payable by Roy's Personal Representatives out of the rest of his estate.

Tax Tip

When we contrast the position of Tom and Jeff's Life Interest Trust in the above example, it becomes apparent that a non-cash gift received personally can be quite onerous. When receiving gifts of any assets which are volatile in nature, such as shares, it is wise to do this through the medium of a Trust, so that it will later be possible to reduce any Inheritance Tax liability which might arise if the value of the gifted asset has fallen.

In the above example, it is interesting to note that the oldest gift within the seven year period did not give rise to any more Inheritance Tax for the recipients of that gift.

However, because this gift used up all of Roy's Nil Rate Band, it had a major impact on the other transferees.

In fact, if the gift to the Wilbury Discretionary Trust had been made more than seven years prior to Roy's death (i.e. just 42 days earlier), the gifts to Bob, Tom and Jeff's Life Interest Trust would all have been covered by the Nil Rate Band and hence free from Inheritance Tax.

Of course, none of us know exactly when we have seven years left to go, but it is worth bearing in mind the fact that gifts in the last seven years of your life will be dealt with chronologically when you die.

Although kind old Roy cannot really be blamed for the final outcome in the example, things might have turned out fairer if he had made some of the smaller gifts first.

Chapter 13

Lifetime Exemptions

There are a number of exemptions available to cover lifetime transfers.

These are absolute exemptions, not dependent on whether you survive for any particular period.

Transfers covered by these exemptions would be free from Inheritance Tax even if you were to pass away the very next day (or even on the way home from the lawyer's office).

These exemptions therefore provide very useful Inheritance Tax planning tools under the right circumstances.

13.1. The Annual Exemption

The first £3,000 of any transfers of value, which are not otherwise exempt, which each individual makes in each tax year are exempt from Inheritance Tax.

Husbands and wives have an annual exemption of £3,000 <u>each</u>.

If the annual exemption is not used one year, it may be carried forward and can be used in the next tax year if that following year's annual exemption is fully exhausted.

Example

Michael makes the following gifts (having never made any before):

2004/2005:	£5,000 to his brother Jermaine
2005/2006:	£4,000 to his brother Tito
2006/2007:	£2,000 to his brother Marlon
2007/2008:	£5,000 to his sister Janet

The first £3,000 of the gift to Jermaine is covered by Michael's annual exemption for 2004/2005.

However, his 2003/2004 annual exemption is also still available, thus covering the remaining £2,000 of this gift. The gift to Jermaine is thus fully exempt from Inheritance Tax.

The unused £1,000 of Michael's 2003/2004 annual exemption is simply lost, as it cannot be carried forward another year.

The first £3,000 of Michael's gift to Tito is covered by his 2005/2006 annual exemption.

The remaining £1,000 of this transfer is thus a Potentially Exempt Transfer.

The gift to Marlon is fully covered by Michael's 2006/2007 annual exemption.

Furthermore, the unused £1,000 of this exemption may be carried forward to 2007/2008.

The first £3,000 of Michael's gift to Janet is covered by his 2007/2008 annual exemption.

The next £1,000 is covered by the unused balance of his 2006/2007 annual exemption. The remaining balance of £1,000 is a Potentially Exempt Transfer.

Tax Tip 1

If Michael were married, he could have avoided the Potentially Exempt Transfers to Tito and Janet by, in each case, first making a gift of £1,000 to his wife who would then have gifted this sum to the ultimate recipient.

Such interim gifts to a spouse must, however, be free of any conditions, so that the spouse would be free to refuse to hand the gift on to the intended recipient if they so wished.

Tax Tip 2

The annual exemption may not be very large, but it is important to bear it in mind when undertaking Inheritance Tax planning.

Making best use of the annual exemption is a matter of timing. The ability to carry it forward one year gives you an effective "second chance", but the use of the annual exemption should nevertheless be reviewed at least every other year.

A married couple who managed to make effective use of the annual exemption in the final few years of their lives would save around £20,000 in Inheritance Tax.

13.2. The Small Gifts Exemption

In addition to the annual exemption, there is also a general exemption for outright gifts of up to £250 to any one person each year.

This exemption applies to any number of such "small gifts" to separate persons each year.

Again, a husband and wife may each utilise this exemption separately in their own right.

Wealth Warning

The small gifts exemption only covers gifts of <u>up to</u> £250. Unlike the annual exemption, it does not cover the first part of a larger gift. Hence, a gift of £251 is not covered by this exemption at all.

It should also be noted that the exemption has to cover all gifts to the same person in the whole tax year.

Furthermore, this exemption cannot be used in conjunction with the annual exemption.

In other words, it is not possible to exempt gifts totalling £3,250 to the same person by using both exemptions together.

Using the Annual and Small Gifts Exemptions

It is, however, possible to combine these two exemptions in order to exempt a number of gifts to different family members.

Used on a cyclical basis, it will also be possible to even out any unfairness.

Example

Chris and Debbie have three sons, Scott, John and Gary, and wish to pass as much wealth on to them as they can by using their annual and small gifts exemptions.

On 5th April 2004, Chris gives Scott £6,000. This is covered by his annual exemptions for 2002/2003 and 2003/2004.

On the same day he also gives £250 each to John and Gary and these gifts are covered by the small gifts exemption.

(Note that care would need to be taken here if other gifts had also been given to the sons earlier in the year – e.g. birthday and Xmas presents.)

At the same time, Debbie gives John £6,000, which is covered by her annual exemptions for 2002/2003 and 2003/2004, and gives £250 each to Scott and Gary.

The next day, 6th April 2004, Chris and Debbie each give £3,000 to Gary. Both of these gifts are covered by their 2004/2005 annual exemptions. Chris and Debbie also each give £250 to Scott and £250 to John.

In the space of 48 hours, Chris and Debbie have managed to give their sons a total of £20,000, which is completely exempt from Inheritance Tax. If they should be unfortunate enough to die within 7 years, this simple strategy will save the family £8,000.

(**NB:** you may notice that Gary has received £250 less than his brothers. This can be evened out again in later years.)

13.3. Gifts in Consideration of Marriage

It's an expensive business when the kids get married, but at least it does provide an extra opportunity to do some Inheritance Tax planning.

Gifts made in consideration of marriage are exempt from Inheritance Tax up to the following limits:

- Parents: £5,000
- Grandparents, Great-Grandparents, etc: £2,500
- Bride to Groom or Groom to Bride: £2,500
- Other Donors: £1,000

All of the above limits apply on an individual basis and the relationships referred to must be to one of the parties to the marriage.

Hence, for example, the groom could receive £5,000 from each of his parents, plus £2,500 from each of his grandparents and £1,000 from all of his aunts and uncles and the bride could receive the same from her family.

Alternatively, the bride's family could make their gifts to the groom or the groom's family could make their gifts to the bride.

Additionally, within this same exemption (and within the same overriding limits as set out above), gifts could be made into a trust for the benefit of:

- The bride and/or groom
- Children of the marriage
- Future spouses of the children of the marriage
- A future spouse of either party to the marriage
- Children of any subsequent marriage of either party to this marriage and future spouses of those children

Gifts in consideration of marriage must be made on or shortly before the marriage in order to fall within the exemption.

The gifts must be fully effective when the marriage takes place. For example, "I give you my property at Blackacre on condition that you marry my daughter."

Where the gifts exceed the limits shown above, the excess may be covered by the annual exemption, if available.

Otherwise they will become Potentially Exempt Transfers unless made to a Discretionary Trust.

13.4. Maintenance of Family

Anything you do for the maintenance of your family is exempted from being a transfer of value for Inheritance Tax purposes.

This is just as well since, otherwise, every time you bought the weekly groceries you would be at risk of causing an Inheritance Tax liability!

This covers expenditure for the maintenance of your spouse, plus any expenditure for the maintenance, education or training of the following persons:

- A child of either you or your spouse who is either under 18 or still in full time education or training on the last 5th April prior to the time of the relevant expenditure.

- Any other child who is not in the care of a parent and is under 18 on the last 5th April prior to the time of the relevant expenditure.

- Any other child who has been in your care for a substantial period and was still in full time education or training on the last 5th April prior to the time of the relevant expenditure.

Your "child" for the purposes of this exemption includes a step-child, adopted child or illegitimate child.

Dependent Relatives

This same exemption also extends to expenditure which represents a reasonable provision for the care or maintenance of a dependent relative.

A "dependent relative" for this purpose is:

i) Your widowed, separated or divorced mother or mother-in-law.

ii) Any other relative of you or your spouse who is incapacitated by old age or infirmity, as a consequence of which they are unable to maintain themselves.

By concession, an unmarried mother may also be included under heading (i) above, as long as she is genuinely financially dependent on the donor, even if she does not qualify as "old or infirm" under heading (ii).

"Old" is usually taken to mean the male state retirement age, i.e. 65.

It can be seen that sexism is alive and well and living in the UK tax legislation. I wonder when we will see a case being taken to the European Court of Justice demanding equal treatment for widowed, separated or divorced fathers?

13.5. Normal Expenditure Out Of Income

Lifetime transfers of value are exempt to the extent that it can be shown:

i) that they are part of the normal, habitual expenditure of the transferor,

ii) that, taking one year with another, they are made out of income (i.e. not out of capital), and

iii) that the transferor is left with sufficient net income to maintain his or her usual standard of living.

This is an extremely useful exemption, since, unlike the annual exemption, there is no financial limit to the amount which can be covered by this exemption if the transferor can afford it.

The amount of gifts or other expenditure involved does not need to be the same every year, as long as it is part of a regular pattern.

All of the following might potentially be covered as long as they meet the three tests set out above:

- Giving your son £10,000 every year.

- Giving your daughter all of your ICI dividends every year.

- Paying your nephew's school fees.

- Buying your brother a new car every three years.

- Paying a monthly life assurance premium on a policy in favour of your daughter.

The last example above is part of a useful Inheritance Tax planning strategy which we will examine further later on in Chapter 19.

Maintaining Your Usual Standard of Living

It has been suggested that the Capital Taxes Office (the Inland Revenue department responsible for policing Inheritance Tax) does not generally question the validity of gifts out of income if they do not, in total, exceed one third of the transferor's net annual income.

Nevertheless, I imagine they would still scrutinise any case where they had reason to think otherwise!

In some circumstances the transferor might reasonably gift a far greater proportion of his or her income and still maintain the usual standard of living, e.g. a very wealthy person with a very frugal lifestyle.

Habitual Gifts

Establishing a gift as being part of your normal, habitual expenditure is a question of fact.

The matter will be determined by looking at the particular facts of each individual case and considering the actual behaviour of the transferor over a number of years.

Naturally, this all only becomes relevant when the transferor has died within seven years of making the gifts concerned.

It is, however, possible to establish that a gift has become part of your normal, habitual expenditure even if you should die after only one such annual gift.

This is because the exemption will still apply if it can be shown that it was the transferor's intention to make the gift every year on an habitual basis.

Tax Tip

Establishing an intention to make a gift on an habitual basis will require some evidence to prove it. For example, if you intend paying your niece's school fees on a regular basis, it would be wise to write a letter to the school confirming this fact.

If you should then unfortunately pass away soon after paying the first set of fees the letter will confirm that this payment was normal habitual expenditure out of income and thus exempt from Inheritance Tax.

Wealth Warning

To be covered by this exemption, the relevant gifts or expenditure must be maintained on a regular basis.

Hence, you must be sure to keep making your "habitual" gifts every year (or such longer period as is your habit). Unlike the annual exemption, there is no scope for carrying this exemption forward!

13.6. Transfers Allowable for Income Tax or Conferring Retirement Benefits

"Transfers of value" which are made for the purposes of a trade, and hence are allowable for Income Tax (or Corporation Tax), are exempt from Inheritance Tax.

This exemption also extends to payments securing pension or other retirement benefits for:

i)   the transferor,
ii) any employee of the transferor, who is not otherwise connected with the transferor, or
iii) the widow, widower or dependants of a person within (ii) above.

Chapter 14

Other Exemptions

In the previous chapter, we looked at Inheritance Tax exemptions which apply only to lifetime transfers. The following further exemptions also apply regardless of whether the gift or transfer is made during the transferor's lifetime or on death (except for the "Death on Active Service" exemption, of course).

In each case, there are a number of exceptions designed to prevent the exemption from being abused.

14.1. Gifts to Charities

Generally, all gifts to charity are exempt from Inheritance Tax. This covers both outright gifts and transfers into a Charitable Trust. A charity is defined as "any body of persons established for charitable purposes only".

Wealth Warning

Foreign charities are excluded!

14.2. Gifts to Housing Associations

Transfers of value which are attributable to land in the UK and are made to registered social landlords are exempt from Inheritance Tax.

14.3. Gifts for National Purposes

Gifts to any of the bodies set out in Appendix F are exempt from Inheritance Tax.

14.4. Gifts to Political Parties

Gifts to qualifying political parties are exempt from Inheritance Tax. To qualify for this exemption the party must, at the last General Election prior to the gift, have:

i)   Two members elected to the House of Commons, or

ii)   One member elected to the House of Commons and also have received not less than 150,000 votes in total.

14.5. Death On Active Service

There is a complete exemption from any Inheritance Tax arising on the death of a person from wound, accident or disease contracted whilst on active service.

A valid certificate issued by the Ministry of Defence is required in support of any claim under this exemption.

Chapter 15

Business & Agricultural Property

Where the appropriate conditions are satisfied, relief from Inheritance Tax is available on the transfer of relevant business property or agricultural property.

As a result, it is now possible to pass on most family businesses free from Inheritance Tax.

Care must be exercised, however, as there are one or two pitfalls awaiting the unwary!

In most cases (and except where noted below), where available, the relief is given at 100%, meaning that the transfer of the business or agricultural property escapes Inheritance Tax altogether.

In those cases where relief is given at a rate less than 100%, the relief is given before applying any other exemptions (such as the annual exemption or Nil Rate Band).

Business Property Relief

Business Property Relief (sometimes known as "BPR" for short) is available on transfers of business property which meet the following three conditions:

i)   The business concerned is a qualifying business,

ii)   The asset itself is relevant business property, and

iii)   The asset has been owned by the transferor for the relevant minimum period.

Qualifying Business

For this purpose, any business is a "qualifying business" as long as it is being carried on with a view to profit and does not consist wholly or mainly of dealing in securities, stocks or shares or land and buildings, nor of making or holding investments (except in the case of the holding company of a trading group). The businesses of "market makers" or "discount houses" on the Stock Exchange do, however, qualify.

Property Businesses

Unfortunately, as is often the case in UK taxation, property businesses are generally not qualifying businesses for this purpose.

Doubtless, those of you with property businesses will think that this is unfair. This is certainly what the Executors of a certain Mr Burkinyoung thought in 1995 when they made a claim for Business Property Relief on the furnished flats he had been letting out on assured shorthold tenancies.

Unfortunately, when they got to Court, the judge told them otherwise, holding that Mr Burkinyoung's properties were only investments and did not constitute a "business" for Inheritance Tax purposes.

The only type of investment properties which are likely to get Business Property Relief are furnished holiday lettings (as explained in the Taxcafe.co.uk guide *"How to Avoid Property Tax"*). That, at least, is accepted to be a "business" for Inheritance Tax purposes. Otherwise, you must be using the property yourself in some sort of trade or profession in order to be able to claim Business Property Relief.

Relevant Business Property

The following types of property may qualify for Business Property Relief:

i)   An interest in an unincorporated business (i.e. a sole trade or profession or a share in a partnership which is carrying on a qualifying business).

ii)   Unquoted shares in a company which is carrying on a qualifying business. For this purpose, "unquoted" includes shares traded in the Alternative Investment Market ("AIM") or the Unlisted Securities Market ("USM").

iii)   Unquoted securities (not shares – e.g. loan stock) of a company when the transferor also has some shares which give him control of that company.

iv)   Quoted shares or securities of a company under the control of the transferor.

v)   Assets held personally by the transferor, but used wholly or mainly for the purposes of the business of a company under their control, or partnership in which they are a partner (or were prior to death in the case of transfers on death).

vi)   Assets held in an Interest In Possession Trust on behalf of the transferor and used wholly or mainly for the purpose of his qualifying business.

Relief under headings (iv) to (vi) is given at only 50%.

Minimum Period

To qualify for Business Property Relief, the relevant property must have been owned by the transferor for a minimum of two years prior to the transfer.

There is an exception to this requirement where the property had replaced other qualifying property and both assets taken together had been owned by the transferor for at least two years out of the five year period preceding the transfer.

When a widow or widower inherits business property, the ownership period for this purpose includes the ownership period of their deceased spouse.

Additionally, the minimum ownership period requirement is ignored when two successive transfers of the same property take place within two years and:

i)   the earlier transfer did qualify for Business Property Relief,

ii)   the second transfer would otherwise qualify for Business Property Relief, and

iii)   at least one of the two transfers occurred on death.

Extra Rules for Lifetime Transfers

Where Business Property Relief applied at the time of a lifetime transfer and the transferor then dies within 7 years, there are some extra conditions which must be satisfied in order for the Business Property Relief to also then apply at the time of the transferor's death.

These are:

i)   The transferee must continue to own either the original assets or suitable replacement assets throughout the period from the date of the original transfer to the date of the transferor's death (or, if earlier, the date of death).

ii)   The original assets themselves (if still owned by the transferee) must continue to be relevant business property for Business Property Relief purposes at the time of the transferor's death.

Heading (ii) above does not apply however, if the original assets were shares or securities which were either:

    a) quoted at the time of the original transfer, or

    b) unquoted throughout the period covered by heading (i) and gave the transferor control of the company immediately prior to the original transfer.

Replacement Business Property

The replacement of relevant business property by other relevant business property has been referred to in a couple of points above.

Broadly this means that on a disposal of the original business property, the same value was reinvested in new qualifying business property. Some detailed conditions do need to be met, however.

Tax Planning with Business Property Relief

Where an individual owns and controls a qualifying trading company, the whole value of that company will effectively be fully exempt from Inheritance Tax.

As that individual nears the end of their life, therefore, it would make sense to ensure that the value of the company is maximised.

Furthermore, any assets held personally by the individual and used in the company's business would only qualify for 50% Business Property Relief.

Again, it might make sense to ensure that these were held in the company.

The potential savings which could be achieved can be illustrated by way of an example.

Example

Madge is a very wealthy and very old woman. Amongst her many assets is her unquoted trading company, Ciccone Ltd. She also owns a CD pressing plant used by the company.

Ciccone Ltd is currently worth £4,000,000. This value takes account of the fact that the company owes £2,000,000 for the purchase of new equipment and also has a bank overdraft of £1,000,000.

The CD pressing plant is worth £10,000,000.

If Madge were to die with things as they stand, her Personal Representatives would be able to claim Business Property Relief.

The calculation would be as follows:

	£
Ciccone Ltd: £4,000,000 @ 100%	*4,000,000*
Pressing Plant: £10,000,000 @ 50%	*5,000,000*
TOTAL	*9,000,000*

Realising that she isn't immortal after all, Madge decides to undertake some Inheritance Tax planning.

She uses part of her substantial private wealth to inject a further £3,000,000 into Ciccone Ltd, thus enabling it to pay off the debt for the new equipment and the bank overdraft.

She also transfers the pressing plant into the company. (If done correctly, this can be done free of both Capital Gains Tax and Stamp Duty Land Tax.)

Ciccone Ltd will now be worth £17,000,000 and the whole of this value will be covered by 100% Business Property Relief.

The overall value of Madge's estate will be virtually unchanged (but see Wealth Warning 1 below). However, this simple piece of planning will save her family £3,200,000 in Inheritance Tax!

Wealth Warning 1

Although the transfer of the pressing plant in the above example can be carried out free of Capital Gains Tax, there could be adverse consequences in the event of an ultimate sale of the property by the company.

Wealth Warning 2

The Inheritance Tax planning undertaken by Madge worked because her company was in debt and was using the pressing plant in its business.

If, on the other hand, she had injected so much capital into the company that it had a surplus in excess of its usual trading requirements, there would have been a restriction on her Business Property Relief.

This is because it would have ceased to be a wholly qualifying company for Business Property Relief purposes. The restriction would have operated by reference to the amount of the "non-trading" surplus as a proportion of the company's total net assets.

If the surplus was large enough, the company might even cease to qualify for Business Property Relief altogether!

Business Property Relief would also be reduced, or possibly lost altogether, if a non-trading asset, such as an investment property, were transferred into the company.

Wealth Warning 3

From a tax perspective, the last thing a dying person should do is sell their business!

The day before the sale, the business would have been completely covered by Business Property Relief and available to be passed on to their family free of Inheritance Tax.

The day after the sale, the sale proceeds would be completely exposed to Inheritance Tax, resulting in the loss of up to 40% in Inheritance Tax.

This is on top of any Capital Gains Tax which arose on the sale. (The Capital Gains Tax could also be avoided if the family sold the business shortly after their death.)

Tax Tip

In practice, unfortunately, it may be necessary to sell the business before the owner's death. Very often, a large proportion of a business's value can be lost when its proprietor dies.

Ideally, business succession planning is something that should be looked at much earlier on, when the original proprietor is still hale and hearty and looking forward to a well-deserved retirement.

However, if a "deathbed sale" type of situation does arise, one way to avoid the pitfalls described above would be to sell the business in exchange for unquoted shares in a trading company. Full Business Property Relief would then be preserved.

Smaller Shareholdings

It is also worth remembering that **any** shareholding in an unquoted trading company qualifies for 100% Business Property Relief. This includes shares in companies listed on AIM or the USM.

The problem is that when one considers the generally volatile nature of unquoted shares, combined with the minimum two year holding period for Business Property Relief, putting your wealth into these type of assets just to avoid Inheritance Tax is a pretty risky business.

Nevertheless, under the right circumstances, it is certainly something to consider. Let's look at an example.

Example
Noel wins a substantial sum on the National Lottery. "Great," his brother Liam says, "how 'bout helpin' me out with me business?"

Noel agrees to give Liam £100,000 to help get his new business started.

However, if Noel simply gives Liam the money, this will be a Potentially Exempt Transfer and if Noel dies within seven years, it will have to be brought back into his estate.

So, what Noel does instead is to subscribe for shares in Liam's company, Wonderwall Ltd. After two years, the Wonderwall shares will qualify and Noel can give them to Liam free from Inheritance Tax. (As long as either Noel lives another seven years or Liam keeps the shares until Noel's death.)

Agricultural Property Relief

Agricultural Property Relief applies in a broadly similar way to Business Property Relief. The following types of property may be covered:

i)   Agricultural land or pasture
ii)   Woodlands
iii)   Buildings used for the intensive rearing of livestock or fish
iv)   Farmhouses, cottages and other farm buildings
v)   Stud farms

Property under (ii) to (iv) must be occupied on a basis ancillary to property also occupied under (i) or (v).

Agricultural Property Relief applies to agricultural land in the UK, the Channel Islands or the Isle of Man. It is given at rates of 50% or 100%, depending on the exact circumstances of the transfer of value arising and subject to the usual raft of provisions designed to prevent abuse.

It is essential that agricultural activities are being carried out on the land at the time of the transfer.

Chapter 16

So Why Not Just Give It All Away?

After reading the chapter on Potentially Exempt Transfers, you may be thinking that avoiding Inheritance Tax should be very simple. All you need to do is to give everything away to your family and then survive for 7 years.

Well, yes, in theory, in the right circumstances, simply giving your property away during your lifetime can be an effective way to avoid Inheritance Tax.

Certainly there is no problem with giving away whatever parts of your estate you can afford to. Just remember to make sure the gifts are Potentially Exempt Transfers (see Chapter 11) and take good care of yourself for seven years. (Or take out some term insurance to cover the Inheritance Tax risk – see Chapter 19.)

Unfortunately, however, in practice, there are a few "catches".

Firstly, any gifts where you retain a beneficial interest in the gifted asset are simply ignored for Inheritance Tax purposes and treated as still being part of your estate.

These types of transfer are known as "Gifts With Reservation". This is particularly a problem when looking at the family home. (But see Chapter 20 for some potential solutions to this problem.)

Secondly, even where a transfer appears to avoid the 'Gifts With Reservation' rules, there may be an Income Tax benefit-in-kind charge applying from 6th April 2005 if the transferor continues to enjoy the use of the asset. (See Chapter 21 for further details.)

Thirdly, when gifting assets other than cash during your lifetime, you may be exposed to Capital Gains Tax.

Most lifetime gifts are treated like a sale at current market value for Capital Gains Tax purposes. (Here there is no problem with the family home, as it is generally exempt from Capital Gains Tax under the Principal Private Residence provisions – these are fully explained in the Taxcafe.co.uk guide *"How to Avoid Property Tax"*.)

Lastly, in practice, you cannot simply give all your assets away because you will need something to live off for the rest of your life! It's fine if you're happy to go and spend the rest of your days in a monastery or a nunnery, or to live off your last £263,000 (for at least seven years) but, in reality, very few people would be happy to follow such a drastic course of action.

Hence, at this point, we need to start looking at some more sophisticated planning options. First, however, we will need to spend a little time looking at that most popular of Inheritance Tax planning tools, the Trust.

Chapter 17

Trusts

There are many different types of Trust, including the following:

- Interest in Possession Trusts

- Life Interest Trusts

- Discretionary Trusts

- Accumulation and Maintenance Trusts

- Disabled Trusts

- Charitable Trusts

In legal parlance (and within the tax legislation) Trusts are generally referred to as "Settlements". The person giving property to the Trust is called the "Settlor", the persons benefiting from the Trust are the "Beneficiaries" and the persons controlling the Trust are the "Trustees".

Very often the Settlor will also be a Trustee. Legally, there is nothing to prevent the Settlor from also being a Beneficiary, although this usually renders the Trust ineffective for Inheritance Tax planning purposes and, from 10th December 2003, can give rise to some unwanted Capital Gains Tax liabilities on the transfers.

The act of transferring an asset into a Trust is known as making a settlement. Thereafter, that asset is known as "Settled Property".

A single Trust may hold some assets which are held on a Discretionary Trust and others which are held on an Interest in Possession Trust.

We looked at Charitable Trusts in Chapter 14 above.

Disabled Trusts and Accumulation and Maintenance Trusts both enjoy privileged treatment for Inheritance Tax purposes and can thus provide very useful planning options when the family's circumstances fit the conditions required to establish these types of Trust.

Very briefly the necessary conditions are:

Accumulation and Maintenance Trusts

i)   One or more of the Trust beneficiaries will become entitled to the Trust assets (or to a life interest therein – see below) on attaining a specified age, not exceeding 25.

ii)   There is no "Interest in Possession" (see below) in any of the Trust assets.

iii)   Income from Trust assets is to be accumulated within the Trust unless applied for the maintenance, education or general benefit of the beneficiaries.

iv)   Either:
   a. No more than 25 years have elapsed since the Trust was established or, if later, first satisfied conditions (i) to (iii), or
   b. All beneficiaries past and present either share a common grandparent or are children, widows or widowers of such persons who died before they would have become entitled as under condition (i) above.

Disabled Trusts

i)   During the life of a disabled person there is no "Interest in Possession" (see below) in any of the Trust assets.

ii)   Not less than half of the funds applied by the Trust during the disabled person's lifetime are applied for the benefit of that disabled person.

iii)   The "disabled person" is:
      a. incapable of managing their own affairs by reason of a mental disorder within the terms of the Mental Health Act,
      b. in receipt of an attendance allowance, or
      c. in receipt of a disability living allowance with a care component at the higher or middle rate.

Interest In Possession Trusts

An Interest In Possession Trust is one where a specific individual is beneficially entitled to all income from, or to otherwise enjoy, the assets of the Trust for a specified period.

Where more than one person is to share the income or enjoyment of the assets for a specified period, this is also an Interest in Possession Trust.

In such cases, the income may be shared in any proportion specified in the Trust Deed.

If, however, the Trustees have discretion over the income paid to the beneficiaries, this would make the Trust a Discretionary Trust (see below).

Example

Nicole transfers a number of investment properties into the All Saints Trust. Under the terms of the Trust, each year's rental profits must be paid to the beneficiaries as follows:

- *Half to Nicole's sister, Natalie*

- *The first £10,000 of the remainder to her friend, Melanie,*

- *The remaining balance to her niece, Shaznay*

Each beneficiary's interest is an Interest In Possession because each of them receives a specific defined amount under the terms of the Trust Deed which is not dependent on the discretion of the Trustees.

Tax Treatment of an Interest In Possession

Whenever a beneficiary has an Interest in Possession they are treated, for Inheritance Tax purposes, as if they owned the asset outright.

Subject to certain exceptions, the termination of their interest, whether on death or otherwise, therefore represents the transfer of the underlying asset for Inheritance Tax purposes.

One of the most important exceptions to this general rule is that, when property reverts to the original Settlor on the termination of an Interest In Possession, the resultant transfer of value is exempt from Inheritance Tax.

We will see how this exception can be put to good use later, in Chapter 20.

Life Interest Trusts

A Life Interest is simply an Interest In Possession where the specified period of the beneficiary's interest is the remainder of their life.

Discretionary Trusts

In the case of a Discretionary Trust, the Trustees have the discretion to decide who to pay the income of the Trust to and who to allow to have the enjoyment of the Trust's assets.

There is a defined class of beneficiaries from whom the trustees can choose (such as "all my grandchildren", for example).

Inheritance Tax Treatment of a Discretionary Trust

Unlike an Interest In Possession Trust, a Discretionary Trust is treated as being a separate and distinct person in its own right for Inheritance Tax purposes.

This is why all transfers of value into a Discretionary Trust are chargeable transfers and not Potentially Exempt Transfers.

A Discretionary Trust's 'separate life' gives rise to some tax planning opportunities, which we will consider further later, in Chapter 22.

Unfortunately, though, to counter this, Discretionary Trusts are subject to an Inheritance Tax charge on every tenth anniversary of their creation.

We'll now examine how this charge is calculated. It gets complex but all will become clear when we work through a practical example at the end.

Ten Year Anniversary Charges

The anniversary charge is calculated as follows:

i)   The value of all relevant property in the Trust on the anniversary date must be calculated. ("Relevant property" means all of the assets held in the Trust excluding any that are, for any reason, exempt from Inheritance Tax.)

ii) To this is added the value of any other property in the Trust on the day that it was transferred into the Trust or, if later, the date that it ceased to be relevant property.

iii) The amount of any non-charitable settlements made into other Trusts on the same day as any settlements into this Trust are also added to this total.

iv) The amount of Inheritance Tax payable on a chargeable lifetime transfer of the total of (i) to (iii) by a hypothetical transferor on the Anniversary Date is calculated taking account of:
   a. The Nil Rate Band, but not any other exemptions, and
   b. Any actual chargeable transfers made by the Settlor in the seven years prior to setting up the Trust (adjusted, as appropriate, for any Potentially Exempt Transfers which became chargeable if that Settlor has died since setting up the Trust).

v)   Using the amount derived at step (iv), the effective rate of Inheritance Tax on the hypothetical lifetime transfer is calculated.

vi) The effective rate is multiplied by 3/10ths and applied to any amounts within (i) above derived from assets which have been held by the Trust throughout the ten year period.

vii)   For any amounts within (i) which are derived from assets held for less than ten years, the charge is reduced by one fortieth for every complete calendar quarter that those assets were not held as relevant assets of the Trust.

Now _that_ calls for an example!

(As usual, exemptions and reliefs other than the nil rate band will be ignored, for the sake of simplicity.)

Example

On 1ˢᵗ April 1995, Mel set up the Spice Discretionary Trust for the benefit of her granddaughters, Emma and Melanie, and any further issue of her children (i.e. any more grandchildren she might have).

She transferred various assets into the Trust at that date. The total value of the assets transferred at that time was £84,000, and hence no Inheritance Tax was payable on Mel's chargeable lifetime transfer.

On the same day, she also transferred £50,000 into an Interest In Possession Trust for her niece Victoria.

Previously, on 25ᵗʰ March 1994, Mel had also given her sister Geri £100,000.

Sadly, Mel passed away in January 2001. (Fortunately, the nil rate band was available to cover all of her lifetime transfers within the previous seven years, which all became chargeable at this time.)

On 1ˢᵗ April 2005, the assets in the Spice Discretionary Trust are worth £300,000.

The anniversary charge is calculated as follows:

	£
Value of relevant property on anniversary date:	*300,000*
Other settlement made on the same day:	*50,000*
Previous chargeable transfers:	*100,000*
(i.e. the Potentially Exempt Transfer to Geri,	
which became chargeable on Mel's death	
in 2001)	
Cumulative total for hypothetical transfer:	**450,000**
Less Nil Rate Band	*263,000*
Gives:	*187,000*
Inheritance Tax at lifetime rate (20%)	**37,400**
Effective rate of Inheritance Tax on the	
hypothetical transfer:	
(£37,400 divided by £300,000 PLUS £50,000,	
expressed as a percentage)	*10.69%*
Rate for anniversary charge:	
3/10ths of 10.69%	*3.21%*
Inheritance Tax Payable:	
3.21% x £300,000	**£9,630**

The result of this rather tortuous calculation is that Inheritance Tax of less than £10,000 is payable on the assets in the Spice Discretionary Trust.

Remember that, had these assets still been in Mel's estate at the time of her death, Inheritance Tax of up to £120,000 would have been payable on them.

Wealth Warning

Transfers of assets out of a Discretionary Trust may also give rise to Inheritance Tax charges.

These "Exit Charges" are broadly based on similar principles to the Ten Year Anniversary Charge. The "Effective Rate" arrived at in each case is multiplied by three tenths, and then also reduced by one fortieth for every complete unexpired calendar quarter remaining before the next Ten Year Anniversary, before being applied to the value of the assets transferred.

For an Exit Charge arising in the first ten year period, the Hypothetical Lifetime Transfer used to derive the Effective Rate is based on the value of the assets in the Trust at its commencement, plus any further settlements made into the Trust between then and the date of the transfer.

Later Exit Charges are based on the Effective Rate applying at the last previous Ten Year Anniversary, as adjusted for any further settlements into the Trust since then.

Chapter 18

How Married Couples Can Double the Nil Rate Band

As explained in Chapter 9, property left to your spouse is usually exempt from Inheritance Tax. However, utilising this exemption to the full is not always necessarily a good idea.

Hence, the first question I ask anyone who comes to me for Inheritance Tax planning advice is "are you married?"

This is because every married couple can save up to £105,200 in Inheritance Tax for their family by following a fairly straightforward planning strategy.

All that this strategy involves is ensuring that the first one of the couple to die uses their Nil Rate Band on transfers which are not made to their widow or widower.

Without this strategy, the couple is simply wasting one of their Nil Rate Bands and thus volunteering to give the Government an extra £105,200!

Example

Remember Arthur from Chapter 6? He died in December 2004, leaving his net estate worth £2,000,000 to his son Tony. Tony ended up with an Inheritance Tax bill of £694,800.

Arthur was, in fact, a widower, and within his estate there was a property worth £263,000, which he had inherited from his wife Doris, who had died in June 2004.

Since Doris left the property to her husband and it was therefore exempt anyway, her Nil Rate Band was never used.

What Doris should have done, instead, was to leave her property to their son, Tony. No Inheritance Tax would have been payable on her death, as her property was covered by the Nil Rate Band.

But when Arthur died later in the year, his estate would have been worth £263,000 less, thus saving £105,200 of Inheritance Tax.

The non-spousal legacy (i.e. the one to Tony in the above example) does not need to be one specific property.

It could be a whole group of assets, or simply worded as a legacy equal to the Nil Rate Band to be paid out of the general assets of the estate.

Tax Tip

When including a non-spousal legacy in your Will with the intention of utilising your Nil Rate Band, it is best not to word it as a legacy of the specific sum which happens to be the current amount of the Nil Rate Band.

What you should do instead is to draft your Will so that it includes a legacy equal to whatever the Nil Rate Band happens to be at the time of your death.

That way, the amount of the legacy will automatically adjust in line with the Nil Rate Band each year.

The non-spousal legacy strategy is pretty simple to follow when, like Arthur and Doris, there are plenty of assets around.

But What if You're Not that Well Off?

The problem for most married couples is that they can't afford to simply give their children £263,000 when one of them dies.

The widow or widower will need to retain sufficient assets to support them for the rest of their life including, in most cases, the family home.

Fortunately, there are some planning strategies available to deal with this dilemma facing the moderately wealthy couple.

The Nil Rate Band Discretionary Will Trust

A method which was very popular a few years ago was for each spouse to set up a Discretionary Trust through their Will (see Chapter 17 for a further explanation of Discretionary Trusts).

Assets at least equal to the Nil Rate Band would be left to the Trust. The surviving spouse would be one of the beneficiaries of the Trust and, in practice, would actually retain all the benefits of ownership of the assets in the Trust.

(This was achieved by ensuring that the Trustees exercised their "discretion" in such a way as to ensure that the surviving spouse received all of the income from, and enjoyment of, the assets.)

These schemes were even sometimes used to pass the deceased's share of the family home into the Discretionary Trust. (See Chapter 20 for some more Inheritance Tax saving strategies for the family home.)

However, the Inland Revenue have recently attacked these types of Discretionary Trusts on the basis that they are really "de facto" Interest In Possession Trusts. This means that the assets of the Trust would remain in the surviving spouse's estate for Inheritance Tax purposes, rendering this planning void.

Nevertheless, the method could probably still be used where the Trust was genuinely discretionary in nature. This would necessitate avoiding the usual "Letter of Instruction" to the

Trustees stating that the surviving spouse is to receive all income from the Trust. It would also be wise to ensure that other beneficiaries did, indeed, receive some Trust income.

The Widow's Loan Scheme

A better method is to leave all (or most) of the assets of the estate to the surviving spouse as specific bequests, but leave a sum equal to the Nil Rate Band to a Discretionary Will Trust.

The surviving spouse would be a beneficiary of the Trust, together with other family members.

The surviving spouse ends up owing a sum equal to the Nil Rate Band to the Trust. What they then do is to simply give an 'IOU' for this amount to the Trust.

When the surviving spouse themselves dies, the amount of the 'IOU' is deductible from their estate, thus doubling the Nil Rate Band!

This scheme has the added strength that the Capital Taxes Office of the Inland Revenue has confirmed that they accept its validity, in principle, for Inheritance Tax purposes, as long as it is done properly.

"Doing it properly" includes drafting the Will very carefully, ensuring that the Trustees have the power to accept IOUs and, above all, getting professional advice!

Chapter 19

Life Assurance & Insurance

One simple way to ensure that your estate is not excessively inflated on your death is to ensure that any Life Assurance policies which you take out are written into Trust for the benefit of other family members.

In that way, the proceeds of the policies will never fall into your estate but will go, instead, to your intended beneficiaries free of Inheritance Tax.

By using a Trust, you will be able to vary the intended beneficiaries over the course of your lifetime.

Ideally, if they can afford to do without it, your spouse should not be the beneficiary under any of your life assurance policies.

As mentioned previously, in Chapter 6, it would be wise to try to get all forms of life insurance cover which you have written into Trust and thus excluded from your estate.

This should also extend to the 'Death Benefit' under any pension schemes, where possible.

Insuring for Inheritance Tax Liabilities

Much of the Inheritance Tax planning discussed elsewhere in this guide depends on the transferor surviving for seven years after a transfer has been made.

When death occurs before the expiry of this period, unexpected tax bills can often arrive as a nasty surprise.

It is often a good idea, therefore, to take out some term life insurance on the transferor to guard against this possibility.

Wealth Warning

Make sure that the transferor themselves is not the beneficiary of the term insurance as this will, once again, inflate the value of their estate and lead to an effective "grossing up" of Inheritance Tax liabilities.

Chapter 20

The Family Home

For most of us, the family home is our major asset and, in many cases, it is also the main cause of Inheritance Tax liabilities (see Chapter 4).

As already mentioned in Chapter 16, the major stumbling block to effective Inheritance Tax planning in respect of the family home is caused by the "Gifts With Reservation" provisions.

Furthermore, whenever the transferor of any asset (but, most particularly, the family home) continues to enjoy the benefit of that asset after 5th April 2005, there will be an Income Tax charge on the deemed 'benefit-in-kind' arising.

The possible application of that charge to the planning methods discussed in this chapter is examined in detail in Chapter 21.

Nevertheless, despite these drawbacks, there are still a number of potential methods for avoiding or reducing the Inheritance Tax on the family home.

Before we proceed to look at some of these methods in detail, it is first important to take a quick look at some legal aspects of Joint Property.

Joint Property

Most couples now own their home jointly. In England and Wales, property held jointly can either be held under a 'Joint Tenancy' or under a 'Tenancy in Common'. A different legal title applies to joint ownership of property in Scotland, but its effect (at least as far as Inheritance Tax planning is concerned) is akin to a 'Tenancy in Common', as described below.

On death, a share in property held under a Joint Tenancy automatically passes to the surviving 'joint tenant'.

This would usually be the widow or widower and is bad Inheritance Tax planning!

A share in property held under a Tenancy in Common may be passed to anyone, under the terms of the deceased's Will.

Hence, whenever undertaking any Inheritance Tax planning on the family home which involves passing a share of the property to anyone other than the surviving spouse, it will first be necessary to ensure that the property is held under a Tenancy in Common and not a Joint Tenancy.

Planning Techniques

20.1. Move Out & Then Give It Away

If you can afford to, and you are willing to do it, you can simply move out of the house and then give it away.

The gift is a Potentially Exempt Transfer which will escape any Inheritance Tax as long as you survive seven years.

Furthermore, as long as you make the gift within three years of the date you move out of the house it will also be exempt from Capital Gains Tax under the Principal Private Residence relief rules.

If you are prepared to do this, you could then move into rented accommodation, or buy a more modest house, with a value below the Nil Rate Band.

This method will not suit everyone, but it is worth considering in some cases.

20.2. The Widow's Loan Scheme

The method described in Chapter 18 above works just as well for the family home as for any other assets. (But see Chapter 21.)

20.3. Leave a Half Share to the Children

You could simply leave your half share in the property to your children, who will then, after your death, own it jointly with your surviving spouse.

As long as the house is not worth in excess of twice the Nil Rate Band, there will be no Inheritance Tax on it on your death.

This is fine as long as you are happy that your children, and, more particularly, their spouses will all get along OK with your spouse after you're gone.

In practice though, this simple route often causes difficulty and families in this situation have been known to come to blows (both metaphorically and physically).

However, there is a way around these practical problems, as follows:

i)   After inheriting a half share in the property, the children set up a Life Interest Trust with their surviving parent as both Trustee and Beneficiary and transfer their share into it.

ii)   The provisions of the Trust are that the property reverts to the children, as Settlors, on the death of the surviving parent.

As explained in Chapter 17 above, when property reverts to the Settlor of a Trust, the transfer is exempt from Inheritance Tax.

Hence, the original half share in the property will get back into the children's hands again free from Inheritance Tax.

Meanwhile, the more recently deceased spouse will have also left the other half share in the property, which they owned absolutely, to the children and their Nil Rate Band will still be available to eliminate, or at least substantially reduce, any Inheritance Tax.

20.4. The "Full Consideration" Method

The 'Gifts with Reservation' rules can be bypassed if, after giving the property to your children, you then pay them a full commercial rent for continuing to live in the property.

Payment of the rent would also help to further reduce your estate for Inheritance Tax purposes.

The major drawback to this method is the fact that your children would have to account for Income Tax on the rent which you are paying to them.

This is likely to render this method impractical in reality in many cases.

20.5. Co-Ownership

This method is very popular with widows and widowers (or other single parents) who have mature single adult children.

Quite simply, you just put the property into joint ownership with one of your children and then live together with them in the house.

The transfer of a half share in the house is a Potentially Exempt Transfer as long as the child is living there.

It is the child's presence in the house which prevents the transfer from being a 'Gift with Reservation'.

20.6. Shearing

The Inheritance Tax on the house can be reduced by dividing up the legal interests in the property in such a way that there is no 'Gift with Reservation'.

Due to anti-avoidance rules, to use this method, the transferor must have owned the property for at least 7 years.

If the property is held jointly by a couple, each of them must have owned their own share for at least 7 years.

The method is most effective when there is no intention of selling the property.

This is how it works:

i)   Create a 299 year lease over the property which becomes effective some years from now (say in 10, 20 or 30 years' time).

ii)   Gift that lease to an Interest In Possession Trust with your children as the beneficiaries and you (and your spouse, if applicable) as trustee.

As the clock runs down towards the time when the lease comes into effect, the value of your freehold interest in the property reduces.

Hopefully, if you time it right, at the time of your death, your interest in the house will have minimal value and will easily be covered by the Nil Rate Band.

What If You Live Too Long?

If you, or your spouse, are fortunate enough to survive long enough to still be around when the lease comes into effect then, in order to avoid the 'Gifts with Reservation' rules, you could start paying a commercial rent to your children (but see 20.4 above re Income Tax).

Alternatively, by that stage, you may well be happy to move into something smaller!

Chapter 21

Income Tax Charges

In his Pre-Budget report on 10th December 2003, the Chancellor of the Exchequer, Gordon Brown, announced proposals to levy an Income Tax charge from 6th April 2005 in circumstances where the donor of any asset continues to benefit from that asset.

Typically, in the case of 'real' property, (i.e. land and buildings), the 'benefit' arises by reason of the fact that the donor continues to live in the property.

The Government refer to such assets as 'pre-owned assets' and, broadly, their intention is to tax the 'annual value' of such assets as a benefit-in-kind on the former owner still enjoying the use of the asset.

Sadly, despite many representations to the contrary, particularly from the accountancy profession, it was confirmed in the Budget on 17th March 2004 that this appalling piece of legislation is to go ahead and will come into force with effect from 6th April 2005 as planned.

The new charge will potentially apply whenever the donor of an asset (i.e. the former legal owner) continues to enjoy the use of it, or otherwise benefit from it, after 5th April 2005.

The annual value on which the charge is based will be the open-market rental for a property, or a fixed percentage of the capital value of most other assets to which the new charge applies.

Any amounts which the former owner is paying for the use of the asset will be deducted from the annual value in arriving at the taxable benefit.

The charge will also apply in cases where the 'donor' has provided the funds to purchase an asset which they enjoy the benefit of after 5th April 2005.

The charge is designed to hit back at a number of Inheritance Tax planning schemes, but will also catch many unintended and innocent victims.

Thankfully, however, there are a few exemptions from this new charge, which will not apply where:

- The asset was gifted before 18th March 1986.

- The asset is owned by the donor's spouse.

- The asset is, in fact, still caught by the Gifts with Reservation Rules for Inheritance Tax purposes (hence, you shouldn't get caught for both taxes on the same asset).

- The asset was sold at an arm's length price for cash (even if to a connected party).

- The donor of the asset had themselves inherited it and their ownership had ceased as a result of a Deed of Variation affecting that inheritance (see Chapter 25).

- The donor's continued enjoyment of the asset is merely incidental or has arisen only as a result of an unforeseen change in family circumstances.

- The annual taxable benefit (after deducting any contributions by the donor, where appropriate) does not exceed £2,500.

Furthermore, the Inland Revenue have confirmed that the charge will not apply where the donor has retained a suitable interest in the asset (such as in the case of a parent who has given a joint share in a property to an adult child who lives with them in that property).

They have also confirmed that the charge should not apply in most cases where a taxpayer has funded life insurance policies held on trust (see Chapter 19).

There is also a 'Get Out Of Jail - But Not Free' card in the shape of an option to elect out of the Income Tax charge, but only by allowing the property to be included back in the donor's estate for Inheritance Tax purposes.

Which takes you straight back to 'Square One' really!

The Implications for Inheritance Tax Planning with the Family Home

Most of the planning techniques outlined in the previous chapter involve a widow or widower having continued enjoyment of their former spouse's share of the property.

At first glance, therefore, the new charge would not seem to apply, as the 'donor' themselves is not around to benefit from the property.

However, there is a bit of a 'fly in the ointment' for anyone who first had to transfer the property from a 'joint tenancy' to a 'tenancy in common' as a preliminary stage in their Inheritance Tax planning.

Technically, where the widow or widower formerly owned the property together with their deceased spouse as joint tenants, they had a share of the ownership of the whole property.

This means that the new Income Tax charge might conceivably apply to their continued occupation of the property after their spouse's death. (But presumably only to the share now owned by their children, or other beneficiaries.)

Tax Tip

When acquiring a new, joint property, this problem might be avoided by making sure that you own it as 'tenants in common' right from the outset.

Unfortunately, since the exact details of the proposed new rules are not yet known, it is not yet possible to assess with any real certainty whether this interpretation of the position will be followed in practice.

Nevertheless, at this stage it is worth us assessing the potential impact of this new charge on the planning techniques described above in Chapter 20:

'Move Out & Then Give It Away' (20.1)

This technique will not be affected by the new rules.

'Widow's Loan Scheme' (when applied to the family home, 20.2)

If the 'IOU' is secured on the property and the widow or widower once jointly owned it with their deceased spouse as 'joint tenants', there is a risk that the new charge will apply.

Payment of interest on the amount of the 'IOU' would alleviate the problem, although the trust itself, would, of course, be taxable on this interest.

It does produce a fairer result though, and perhaps something which you could live with.

Tax Tip

If following this strategy, it would only be necessary to pay enough interest to keep the taxable benefit below the de minimis threshold of £2,500.

'Leave A Half Share To The Children' (20.3)

As outlined above, a charge may arise under this method if the surviving parent was previously a 'joint tenant' with their deceased spouse.

The 'Full Consideration' Method (20.4)

This method is unaffected by the new charge, owing to the fact that the donor of the property is making full payment for their continued use of it.

'Co-Ownership' (20.5)

The Inland Revenue have specifically confirmed that this method will not be caught under the new charge.

'Shearing' (20.6)

At present, I would not expect this method to be affected by the new charge, since the donor(s) continue to retain ownership of the property.

Payment of a full commercial rent would be necessary once the lease comes into effect.

Tax Charges & Domicile

For UK Domiciled taxpayers (see Chapter 26), the charge applies to any relevant assets worldwide.

For non-domiciled, but UK resident, taxpayers, it will apply only to any relevant UK assets.

For anyone who did not have a UK 'Domicile of Origin' (see Chapter 26), but who has subsequently acquired actual or deemed UK Domicile, the charge will not apply to any non-UK assets which they ceased to own before acquiring UK Domicile.

Chapter 22

Tax Planning With Discretionary Trusts

Because Discretionary Trusts are separate persons for Inheritance Tax purposes, they provide the opportunity to shelter assets in a vehicle which exists outside of any individual person's estate. (Subject, of course, to the Anniversary and Exit charges explained in Chapter 17).

In effect, and subject to any other transfers which you may be making, there is the opportunity to transfer assets free from Inheritance Tax into Discretionary Trusts every seven years which are equal in value to the Nil Rate Band.

For a couple, that amounts to over £525,000 which may be safeguarded from Inheritance Tax in every seven year period.

Wealth Warning

When using Discretionary Trusts for Inheritance Tax planning, it is important to ensure that it is impossible for either the transferor or their spouse to benefit from the Trust.

Otherwise, the "Gift with Reservation" rules will apply, thus rendering the Trust ineffective for Inheritance Tax purposes.

Furthermore, from 10th December 2003, this is also imperative from a Capital Gains Tax perspective.

From that date onwards, the general Capital Gains Tax holdover relief for gifts into such a Trust (see below) ceases to be available where the settlor (or their spouse) is able to benefit in any way from the recipient Trust.

Such a gift would therefore now give rise to an immediate Capital Gains Tax charge in most cases.

Tax Tip

Due to the ten year anniversary charges, it is usually wise to ensure that some or all of the property in the Trust comes back out of the Trust, and into the hands of the ultimate beneficiaries, within ten years of the original transfer.

As long as care has been exercised over the amounts of chargeable transfers made in the seven years prior to setting up the Trust (and in setting up the Trust itself), there should be no Inheritance Tax 'Exit Charges' within this first ten-year period.

This means that up to ten years of 'capital growth' in the value of the Trust assets can accumulate free from Inheritance Tax.

Wealth Warning

You should also avoid making any other settlements on the same day as setting up the Trust. (See Chapter 17.)

Why Not Just Give Assets Directly To The Beneficiaries?

The further added extra advantage which Discretionary Trusts provide is the ability to "hold over" any Capital Gains arising on the assets transferred.

Remember that, in the case of a direct gift to another individual (or to an Interest In Possession Trust), the transferor is deemed to have disposed of the asset at its current market value, and must pay Capital Gains Tax accordingly.

However, because a gift into a Discretionary Trust is a Chargeable Lifetime Transfer (see Chapter 10), the transferor is allowed to claim to "hold over" their gain for Capital Gains Tax purposes.

What this means is that no Capital Gains Tax is payable on the transfer and the Trust is treated, for Capital Gains Tax purposes, as having acquired the asset at the same price as that originally paid by the transferor.

Furthermore, when, at a later date, the Trust then transfers the asset to the ultimate beneficiary, the Trustees and the beneficiary may, once again, claim that the Capital Gain should be "held over".

Hence, by this method, appreciating assets may be passed on free of both Inheritance Tax and Capital Gains Tax.

Chapter 23

Reversionary Interest Trusts

Reversionary Interest Trusts

Another very useful type of Trust in Inheritance Tax planning is the Reversionary Interest Trust.

This name is a slight misnomer, because, what is actually involved is not one single Trust, but a series of smaller Trusts.

What happens is that the transferor gives a substantial sum to the Reversionary Interest Trust, which is then divided up amongst a series of smaller Trusts.

Each of the smaller Trusts is an Interest In Possession Trust. The original transfer is thus a Potentially Exempt Transfer, which will be exempt from Inheritance Tax when the transferor has survived for seven years.

The small Trusts then carry the following rights:

Trust 1: income to the Interest In Possession beneficiary for one year, after which the remaining funds in the Trust are paid to the original transferor.

Trust 2: income to the Interest In Possession beneficiary for two years, after which the remaining funds in the Trust are paid to the original transferor.

Trust 3: income to the Interest In Possession beneficiary for three years, after which the remaining funds in the Trust are paid to the original transferor.

And so on …

The effect of this is that the transferor continues to receive an "income" stream from their investment, despite the fact that much of it is no longer in their estate for Inheritance Tax purposes.

(The statistical value of their reversionary interests in the Trusts does still have to be included in their estate, but this will steadily reduce as time passes.)

Actually, what the transferor is receiving is not, strictly speaking, income at all, but a return of capital.

This therefore has the added advantage of being free from Income Tax too!

Chapter 24

Gift/Loan Trusts

Yet another variation on the Trust theme is a 'Gift/Loan' Trust.

Under this method, the donor's original gift into the trust is progressively turned into a loan, so that the original value may be withdrawn to help maintain the donor in their old age.

Meanwhile, the capital growth and accumulated income within the trust is passed on to the donor's beneficiaries and is thus kept out of the donor's estate.

This complex structure requires detailed professional help to set up.

Chapter 25

Deeds of Variation

Perhaps the "last resort" in Inheritance Tax planning is the Deed of Variation.

Despite rumours to the contrary, the ability to execute such Deeds, varying the terms of a deceased person's Will, still remains with us.

Deeds of Variation are an essential planning tool where a family finds that the terms of the deceased's Will (or intestacy) have an undesired effect for Inheritance Tax purposes.

Where all of the beneficiaries are in agreement, it is possible to vary the Will in order to create a better Inheritance Tax result (e.g. to utilise the deceased's Nil Rate Band).

Conditions

i)   The required variations must be recorded in writing within two years of the death (this is the Deed).

ii)   All those persons who were original beneficiaries under the Will or intestacy, and any other persons who benefit from the variations, should sign the Deed.

iii)   An election must then be made in writing to the Inland Revenue within six months after the date of the Deed by the persons in (ii) above and, if the variation results in additional Inheritance Tax becoming payable, the deceased's Personal Representatives.

iv) The variation must not be made for any consideration in money or money's worth, except in the case of other compensatory variations to the deceased's Will or intestacy.

Variations made by such a Deed are treated for Inheritance Tax purposes as if they had been made by the Deceased.

This means that a widow or widower who becomes a party to a Deed of Variation and, as a result, gives up a right to a part of their inheritance, is not themselves regarded as having made any transfer of value (neither chargeable nor otherwise).

Chapter 26

Domicile

In essence, your "Domicile" is the country which you consider to be your permanent home.

This does not necessarily equate to your country of birth, nor to the country in which you happen to be living at present.

Furthermore, "Domicile" should not be confused with residence, which is a far more transitory concept (but see Chapter 5 above regarding deemed domicile).

At this point, it is worth noting that, technically speaking, you cannot actually have "UK Domicile" but will, instead, have your domicile in England and Wales, Scotland or Northern Ireland.

However, there are very few instances where this actually makes any practical difference so, throughout the rest of this guide, I have simply referred to "UK Domicile".

More importantly, it is also worth noting that the Channel Islands and the Isle of Man are not part of the UK for tax purposes, including Inheritance Tax and Domicile.

Domicile of Origin

At birth, each person acquires the "Domicile" of the person on whom they are legally dependent at that time. That person will, in most cases, be their father, but it is their mother, if either:

i) Their father is dead at the time of their birth, or

ii) Their parents are both alive, but living apart, and they have a home with their mother, but do not have a home with their father.

The domicile which you acquire at birth is known as your "Domicile of Origin".

Throughout your minority, you continue to have the same Domicile as the person on whom you are legally dependent.

You only become capable of having your own independent domicile when you reach whichever of the following ages is applicable, or marry under that age. The applicable ages are:

i) In England, Wales and Northern Ireland, the age of 16.
ii) In Scotland, for a boy, the age of 14.
iii) In Scotland, for a girl, the age of 12.

Example

Farouk was born in Zanzibar in 1946. He lived with both of his unmarried parents at that time. His father was domiciled in India and his mother was domiciled in Tanzania. Farouk therefore acquired Indian domicile at birth and this was his Domicile of Origin.

In 1960, Farouk's mother left his father, taking Farouk with her, and moved to England. She did not intend to make the UK her permanent home, however, and intended to return to Tanzania when circumstances permitted.

At this point, Farouk therefore acquired Tanzanian domicile (i.e. his mother's). This became his new Domicile of Origin. (Your Domicile of Origin can only change during your minority; once you have become capable of having your own independent domicile (see above), it cannot be changed.)

Assuming this position continued until his 16th birthday, Farouk would then acquire a final Domicile of Origin of Tanzania.

Domicile of Choice

In most cases, a person's Domicile of Origin remains their Domicile for the rest of their life.

This Domicile can only be changed, to a "Domicile of Choice", through permanent emigration (and, in this case, I <u>mean</u> permanent).

Acquiring a new domicile for tax purposes, as a "Domicile of Choice", can be very difficult to prove. This is both good news and bad news since it cuts both ways and the Inland Revenue have had just as much difficulty proving that a taxpayer has acquired the UK as his Domicile of Choice as taxpayers have had in proving that they have acquired a Domicile somewhere else.

To acquire a new Domicile, as a Domicile of Choice, it is necessary to not only demonstrate an intention to adopt the new country as your permanent home, but also to follow this up by action and subsequent conduct.

If the taxpayer abandons their Domicile of Choice, their Domicile automatically reverts to their Domicile of Origin.

Example

Brian is UK Domiciled. However, in 2004, he decides to emigrate permanently to Australia and thus become Australian Domiciled.

He declares this intention on form P85, which he lodges with the UK Inland Revenue shortly before he departs for Sydney.

In 2007, Brian gets a terrific offer to work in California, so he leaves Australia to adopt the USA as his new permanent home.

Brian's Domicile has now reverted to the UK!

Wealth Warning

If you intend to emigrate to avoid UK Inheritance Tax, make sure you pick the right country first time!

Although Brian might eventually be able to establish US Domicile, this will now be very difficult for him because he has established a "track record" of abandoning his so-called "permanent home".

How now could he possibly prove that he has no intention of ever returning to the UK?

Wealth Warning Part 2

The other point to note about emigrating to avoid Inheritance Tax is that you will also be _deemed_ to be UK Domiciled at the time of your death if you were actually still UK Domiciled under general principles at any time in the preceding three years.

(As before, this may be affected by one of the Double Tax Treaties referred to in Appendix B.)

Emigrating for this purpose must therefore be done early and carefully.

Establishing a Domicile of Choice (AKA "Emigrating")

There is no set procedure for establishing a Domicile of Choice.

Like many things in the tax world, each individual case will be examined on its own particular merits.

Here, however, are a few practical tips to follow:

- Declare your intentions to the Inland Revenue on form P85 before leaving the UK (see Appendix C).

- Buy a home in your new country.

- Take your family with you.

- Take whatever steps you can to establish citizenship, nationality, etc, in your new country.

- Take up employment in your new country (or, alternatively, establish your own business there).

- Get on the electoral roll in your new country.

- Buy a grave plot in your new country (this is given a great deal of importance by the tax authorities when looking at Domicile).

- Try to visit the UK as little as possible.

- Sell as many UK assets as you can.

- Resign membership of any clubs, associations, etc, in the UK.

- Write a Will in your new country.

- DO NOT MOVE ON AGAIN TO ANOTHER COUNTRY!

Retaining a Domicile of Origin

If you are lucky enough to have a non-UK Domicile of Origin it is far, far, easier to retain this as your Domicile than it is to acquire a Domicile of Choice.

As stated above, it is very difficult for the Inland Revenue to prove that an individual has acquired a new Domicile of choice.

This is especially true if the individual themselves states that it is their intention to return to their country of origin one day.

In this case, an "intention" does not have to be backed up by action.

Example

Anita was born in France, of French parents. She has, however, lived in the UK for over 40 years, having moved here in her early twenties. Despite this, she has always stated that she intends to return "home" before she dies.

Anita remains French Domiciled.

(However, as explained above, she would be deemed to be UK Domiciled for Inheritance Tax purposes, as she has been resident here for at least 17 of the last 20 years – subject to the UK/France Double Tax Treaty.)

Tax Tip

If you have a foreign Domicile of Origin, it is worth retaining this for UK tax purposes.

To ensure that you don't end up with deemed UK Domicile for Inheritance Tax purposes, you should try to spend four years out of every twenty abroad (or one in five, if you prefer).

This does not have to be in the same country as your Domicile of Origin.

You should also complete a form DOM 1, declaring yourself to be non-Domiciled, and submit it to the Financial Intermediaries and Claims Office (see Appendix C).

When completing your Tax Return, you should tick the boxes in Question 9 on page 2 of your Tax Return and complete pages NR1 and NR2 as appropriate.

Finally, it may be worth buying a grave plot in the country which is your Domicile of Origin. This is accepted as a very strong indication of your intention to return to that country at some future date.

Domicile and Marriage

Marriage does not affect a man's Domicile and it never has.

For women married on or after 1st January 1974, marriage again has no affect on their Domicile.

For women married before 1st January 1974, the position is as follows:

- Non-US Nationals:
  You adopt your husband's Domicile at the date of marriage. If this changed at any time before 1st January 1974, and you were still married and not legally separated at that time, then yours will have changed with his. You will continue to have the same Domicile as you thus had on 1st January 1974 unless you have subsequently adopted a new Domicile of Choice, or re-adopted your Domicile of Origin in the same way as anyone else would adopt a Domicile of Choice.

- US Nationals:
  Your Domicile is now unaffected by your marriage. (Prior to 6th April 1976 the rules for non-US Nationals as above would have applied if you had married before 1st January 1974.)

Appendix A

Inheritance Tax Exemptions 2004/2005

Nil Rate Band:	**£263,000**
Transfers To Non-Domiciled Spouse:	**£55,000**
Annual Exemption:	**£3,000***
Small Gifts Exemption:	**£250**

Gifts in consideration of marriage:

Parents:	**£5,000**
Grandparents, etc:	**£2,500**
To Each other:	**£2,500**
Other Donors:	**£1,000**

*NB: 2003/2004 annual exemption of £3,000 may be added if not previously utilised and 2004/2005 annual exemption is exhausted.

Appendix B

Double Tax Treaties

Countries with which the UK has Double Tax Treaties covering Inheritance Tax (and its overseas equivalents).

- **France**
- **Irish Republic**
- **India**
- **Italy**
- **Netherlands**
- **Pakistan**
- **South Africa**
- **Sweden**
- **Switzerland**
- **USA**

Appendix C

Useful Addresses

Where relevant, forms P85 or DOM 1 should be sent to:

Inland Revenue
Financial Intermediaries and Claims Office*
St John's House
Merton Road
Bootle
Merseyside
England
L69 9BB

(Tel: +44 151 472 6196)

* Also known as "FICO"

Appendix D

Connected Persons

Connected persons include the following:

- Husband or wife (but note that such transfers are usually exempt)
- Mother, father or remoter ancestor
- Son, daughter or remoter descendant
- Brother or sister
- Mother-in-law, father-in-law, son-in-law, daughter-in-law, brother-in-law or sister-in-law
- Business partners
- Companies under the control of the other party to the transaction or of any of his/her relatives as above
- Trustees of a trust where the other party to the transaction, or any of his/her relatives as above, is a beneficiary.

Appendix E

Example Documentation

<u>1. Memorandum recording a gift (Inheritance Tax liability remains with transferor)</u>

MEMORANDUM OF GIFT FROM

Roger Meadows of 3 Taylor Street, Penzance

TO

Ian Deacon of 4 Queen Street, Belfast

MEMORANDUM that on 15th May 2004 Roger Meadows transferred by way of gift to Ian Deacon the sum of £1,000,000.

Dated: 20th May 2004

Signed by Roger Meadows:

Signed by Ian Deacon:

<u>2. Memorandum recording transferee's liability for Inheritance Tax on a lifetime transfer</u>

MEMORANDUM OF GIFT FROM

James Stewart of 15 Castle Street, Stirling

TO

Mary Stewart of 42 Palace Road, Linlithgow

MEMORANDUM that on 16th May 2004 James Stewart transferred by way of gift to Mary Stewart (subject to the payment of any

Inheritance Tax) the assets listed in the schedule below to the intent that they have become and are the absolute property of Mary Stewart and IN CONSIDERATION of such transfer Mary Stewart undertook to pay any Inheritance Tax in respect of such gift assessed upon James Stewart or his Personal Representatives and indemnifies James Stewart and his Personal Representatives accordingly.

SCHEDULE

- Property at 87 Flodden Avenue, Berwick upon Tweed
- 10,000 Ordinary £1 Shares in Darnley plc
- The sum of £5,000 in cash

Dated: 21st May 2004

Signed by James Stewart:

Signed by Mary Stewart:

Appendix F

National Bodies

Subject to certain anti-avoidance provisions, gifts to any of the following bodies are exempt from Inheritance Tax:

- The National Gallery
- The British Museum
- The National Museum of Scotland
- The National Museum of Wales
- The Ulster Museum
- Other similar institutions approved for this purpose by HM Treasury
- Other Museums or Art Galleries in the UK which are maintained by a local authority or UK University.
- Any library whose main function is to provide teaching and research facilities for a UK University.
- The Historic Buildings and Monuments Commission for England
- The National Trust
- The National Trust for Scotland
- The National Art Collections Fund
- The Trustees of the National Heritage Memorial Fund
- The Friends of the National Libraries
- The Historic Churches Preservation Trust
- Nature Conservancy Council for England
- Scottish National Heritage
- Countryside Council for Wales
- Any Local Authority
- Any Government Department
- Any University (or University College) in the UK
- Certain Health Service Bodies

Need Affordable & Expert Tax Planning Advice?

Try Our Unique Question & Answer Service

The purpose of this guide is to provide you with detailed guidance on Inheritance Tax issues.

Ultimately you may want to take further action or obtain advice personal to your circumstances.

Taxcafe.co.uk has a unique online tax advice service that provides access to highly qualified tax professionals at an affordable rate.

No matter how complex your question, we will provide you with detailed tax planning guidance through this service. The cost is just £69.95.

To find out more go to **www.taxcafe.co.uk** and click the Tax Questions button.

Pay Less Tax!

... with help from Taxcafe's unique tax guides, software and Q&A service

All products available online at **www.taxcafe.co.uk**

➢ **How to Avoid Property Tax.** Essential reading for property investors who want to know all the tips and tricks to follow to pay less tax on their property profits.

➢ **Using a Property Company to Save Tax.** How to massively increase your profits by using a property company... plus all the traps to avoid.

➢ **How to Avoid Inheritance Tax.** A-Z of Inheritance Tax planning, with clear explanations & numerous examples. Covers simple & sophisticated tax planning.

➢ **Non Resident & Offshore Tax Planning.** How to exploit non-resident tax status to reduce your tax bill, plus advice on using offshore trusts and companies.

➢ **Incorporate & Save Tax.** Everything you need to know about the tax benefits of using a company to run your business.

➢ **Bonus vs Dividends.** Shows how shareholder/directors of companies can save thousands in tax by choosing the optimal mix of bonus and dividends.

➢ **Selling a Business.** A potential minefield with numerous traps to avoid but significant tax saving opportunities.

➢ **How to Claim Tax Credits.** Even families with higher incomes can make successful tax credit claims. This guide shows how much you can claim and how to go about it.

➢ **Property Capital Gains Tax Calculator.** Unique software that performs complex Capital Gains Tax calculations in seconds.

➢ **Fast Tax Advice**. We offer a unique Tax Question Service. Answers from highly qualified specialist tax advisers. Just click the Tax Questions button on our site.

Essential Property Investment Guides

...written by leading experts and packed with tips & tricks of the trade

All products available online at **www.taxcafe.co.uk**

➤ **An Insider's Guide to Successful Property Investing.** Little-known secrets of successful property investors. A "must read" for anyone interested in making big profits and avoiding costly mistakes.

➤ **An Insider's Guide to Successful Property Investing - Part II.** How the experts make millions by using simple but clever techniques to find, buy, manage and sell property.

➤ **No Money Down Property Millions.** Written by a wealthy property investor, this entertaining and brilliantly clever guide shows you how to invest in property without using any of your own money.

➤ **The Successful Landlord's Handbook.** Definitive guide for Buy to Let investors. Covers: sourcing cheap property, using borrowed money to earn big capital gains, finding quality tenants, earning high rents, legal traps, letting agents, and lots more...

➤ **63 Common Defects in Investment Property & How to Spot Them.** With full colour illustrations, this unique guide will save you thousands by steering you clear of no-hope property investments and towards bargain-priced gems.

➤ **Property Auctions Bargains.** One of the best-kept secrets of successful property investors is to buy at rock-bottom prices at auction. This A-Z guide tells you everything you need to know.

www.taxcafe.co.uk

DISCLAIMER BY TAXCAFE UK LIMITED

1. Please note that this Tax Guide is intended as general guidance only for individual readers and does NOT constitute accountancy, tax, investment or other professional advice. Further general tax guidance on circumstances not covered in this Tax Guide can be obtained through the TAXCafe™ online "Question and Answer Service which is available at www.taxcafe.co.uk. Taxcafe UK Limited accepts no responsibility or liability for loss which may arise from reliance on information contained in this Tax Guide.

2. Please note that tax legislation, the law and practices by government and regulatory authorities (e.g. the Inland Revenue) are constantly changing and the information contained in this Tax Guide is only correct as at the date of publication. We therefore recommend that for accountancy, tax, investment or other professional advice, you consult a suitably qualified accountant, tax specialist, independent financial adviser, or other professional adviser. Please also note that your personal circumstances may vary from the general examples given in this Tax Guide and your professional adviser will be able to give specific advice based on your personal circumstances.

3. This Tax Guide covers UK taxation only and any references to "tax" or "taxation" in this Tax Guide, unless the contrary is expressly stated, refers to UK taxation only. Please note that references to the "UK" do not include the Channel Islands or the Isle of Man. Foreign tax implications are beyond the scope of this Tax Guide.

4. Whilst in an effort to be helpful, this Tax Guide may refer to general guidance on matters other than UK taxation, Taxcafe UK Limited are not experts in these matters and do not accept any responsibility or liability for loss which may arise from reliance on such information contained in this Tax Guide.

5. Please note that Taxcafe UK Limited has relied wholly on the expertise of the author in the preparation of the content of this Tax Guide. The author is not an employee of Taxcafe UK Limited but has been selected by Taxcafe UK Limited using reasonable care and skill to write the content of this Tax Guide.

Printed in the United Kingdom
by Lightning Source UK Ltd.
102222UKS00003B/118-204